ABORTION SERVICES AND REPRODUCTIVE JUSTICE

IN RURAL SOUTH AFRICA

ABORTION SERVICES AND REPRODUCTIVE JUSTICE

IN RURAL SOUTH AFRICA

Ulandi du Plessis
Catriona Ida Macleod

WITS UNIVERSITY PRESS

Published in South Africa by:
Wits University Press
1 Jan Smuts Avenue
Johannesburg 2001

www.witspress.co.za

First published 2024

http://dx.doi.org.10.18772/12024038738

978-1-77614-873-8 (Paperback)
978-1-77614-874-5 (Hardback)
978-1-77614-875-2 (Web PDF)
978-1-77614-876-9 (EPUB)

This publication is peer reviewed following international best practice standards for academic
and scholarly books.

Project manager: Catherine Damerell
Copy editor: Lisa Compton
Proofreader: Alison Paulin
Indexer: Marlene Burger
Cover design: Hybrid Creative
Typeset in 11 point Minion Pro

This book is dedicated to all those women and gender queer people who have been denied abortions, especially in rural areas.

CONTENTS

LIST OF FIGURES AND TABLES   ix

ACKNOWLEDGEMENTS   xi

ABBREVIATIONS AND ACRONYMS   xiii

NOTE ON TERMINOLOGY   xv

INTRODUCTION   Setting the Scene   1

CHAPTER 1   'If it is Legal These Days, I Do Not Know': Knowledge of Abortion Legislation and Services   21

CHAPTER 2   Aborting a Pregnancy: The Complexity of the Decision-Making Process   39

CHAPTER 3   Sin, Injury and Discord: Community Attitudes and Understandings of Abortion   56

CHAPTER 4   'And the Story Spread': Abortion Stigma in Rural South Africa   78

CHAPTER 5   Barriers to Having an Abortion in Rural South Africa   97

CHAPTER 6   The Conundrum of Confidentiality Versus Cost: Abortion Service Provision Preferences   114

CONCLUSION   Implications and Future Directions   129

NOTES   145

BIBLIOGRAPHY   159

INDEX   173

FIGURES AND TABLES

INTRODUCTION

Figure 0.1   Map of study sites in the Eastern Cape   11

Figure 0.2   Research steps in the DCE   15

Figure 0.3   Example of a choice task   16

Table 0.1   Demographic characteristics of the DCE sample   17

CHAPTER 1

Figure 1.1   Abortion advert posted on a street in the Eastern Cape   28

CHAPTER 6

Figure 6.1   First and second preferences of factors in choosing an
             abortion services provider   116

Figure 6.2   First and second preferences for type of abortion services provider 118

Figure 6.3   First preference for source of abortion information   126

Table 6.1   MLR coefficients for services offered (pooled sample and by sex)   120

Table 6.2   MLR coefficients for services offered by site   120

Table 6.3   MLR coefficients for facility location (pooled sample and by sex)   122

Table 6.4   MLR coefficients for facility location by site   123

Table 6.5   MLR coefficients for opening times (pooled sample and by sex)   124

Table 6.6   MLR coefficients for opening times by site   125

Table 6.7   Ranking of sources of information about abortion   126

CHAPTER 7

Figure 7.1   Reparative reproductive justice dimensions in relation
             to abortion care   130

ACKNOWLEDGEMENTS

The data used in this book were collected during a study funded by Marie Stopes South Africa (MSSA). The authors would like to thank Marie Stopes and their very supportive team, including Martha Nicholson, Sakhile Mhlongo, Kovilin Govender, Whitney Chinogwenya, Chelsey Porter and Ashveer Doolam. At different stages of the project, colleagues and students at the Critical Studies in Sexualities and Reproduction (CSSR) provided input and assisted with the project. We thank the CSSR team, specifically Jabulile Mary-Jane Jace Mavuso and Agnes Sanyangore. We partnered with local NGOs in the process of collecting data. We thank Keiskamma Trust and Bulungula Incubator for putting their resources at our disposal. The Health Programme Managers of these NGOs, Keiskamma Trust and Bulungula Incubator, Nomthandazo Manjezi and Bongezwa Maleyile, respectively, provided invaluable project input and served on our expert panel. Their health worker teams helped us gather the quantitative data and supported our fieldworkers while they were doing interviews. We do not name them directly here but have thanked them personally. The following individuals provided excellent contributions: Shabnam Shaik, Jamie Alexander and Ziyanda Ntlokwana with the fieldworker training and fieldworker coordination, Erofili Grapsa and Matthew Quaife with the statistics and experimental design, and Megan Reuvers and Sean van Eeden with the graphic design. At the CSSR, we endeavour to involve Rhodes University students in our projects. This way, they can gain valuable research skills while making extra money. The following students did an excellent job collecting data in the field: Amanda Kepe, Siphosethu Matiwana, Noludwe Makwetu, Ncebakazi Makwetu, Qhawekazi Mahlasela, Wongeswa August, Maliviwe Mhlaba, Lusanda Jaden, Chumano Mpupha, Siyachuma Sintu, Aviwe Dikeni, Lithalethu Hashe, Thab'sile Mgwili and Sinethemba Leve. A special thanks also to our transcribers and translators: Angelinah Dazela, Kholisa Podile, Akha Tutu, Amahle Mtsekana, Amanda Kepe, Andisiwe Barnabas, Andiswa Bukula, Anelisa Kona, Athenkosi Skoti, Athule Zabo, AvelaOnke Nyathela, Aviwe Dikeni, Aviwe Khanya May, Azole Sindelo, Bamanye Lwana, Bamanye Saki, Buhle Majavu, Bulelani Mkula, Bulelani Nonyukela, Busisiwe Klaas, Chumano Mpupha, Dabula Maxam, Duduzile Molefe-Khamanga, Esona Madikwa, Jeremia Lepheana, Khuselwa Anda Tembani, Lithalethu Hashe, Lusanda Jaden Goba, Lwandisa Pinyana, Maliviwe Mhlaba, Malixole Ntlokwana, Mihlali Mbunge, Mihle Bango, Mpendulo Siphika, Mziwonke Qwesha, Nandipha Maliti, Nasipi Mtsi, Ncebakazi Makwetu, Neliswa Maqanda, Noludwe Makwetu, Nonkosi Matrose, Ntobeko Qolo, Phiwokuhle Tom, Phiwokuhle Yase, Pura Lavisa, Qhawekazi Mahlasela, Sandile Saki, Sandisiwe Mafalala, Simbongile Phumza Calana, Sinazo Menzelwa, Sinoxolo Skeyi, Siphamandla Mceleli, Siphosethu Matiwana, Siyachuma Sintu, Tabisa Booi, Thab'sile Mgwili, Thapelo Siyasanga Zane Ngesi, Thasky Fatyi, Thato Tlakedi, Thulani Ntisana, Tsepiso Nzayo, Tuleka Ngincane, Wongezwa August, Yamkela Ntshkaza, Yanga Mtshawu Gqweya, Zikho Dana, Ziyanda Ntlokwana, Zintle Tsholwana, Zodwa Mtirara and Zukiswa Maqoko.

ABBREVIATIONS AND ACRONYMS

ANC	African National Congress
CTOP Act	Choice on Termination of Pregnancy Act No. 92 (1996)
DCE	discrete choice experiment
DEDEAT	Department of Economic Development, Environmental Affairs and Tourism
ECARP	East Cape Agricultural Research Project
HIV	human immunodeficiency virus
MLR	multinomial logistic regression
MSSA	Marie Stopes South Africa
NGO	non-governmental organisation
SADHS	South African Demographic and Health Survey
TOP	termination of pregnancy
VCAT	value clarification and attitude transformation
WHO	World Health Organization

NOTE ON TERMINOLOGY

People with uteri who require abortion services are not necessarily cisgender women. Transgender men, intersex people and gender queer people may conceive and decide on an abortion. However, our study and many others we cite concentrate on cisgender women. On this basis, we should, strictly speaking, add 'cisgender' in front of the words 'woman' and 'women' throughout the book. This makes for cumbersome reading, however. We thus declare upfront that we use 'woman' and 'women' to refer to cisgender women. Other people with uteri will face similar challenges to cisgender women in accessing abortion services in these rural areas and others, which, unfortunately, we do not cover in this book.

INTRODUCTION: SETTING THE SCENE

For us in the rural areas, we have to fight 20 or 30 times more to get services compared to our urban counterparts. Here in Engcobo, one of the
youth who wanted to have an abortion had to walk far to the nearest
service provider, which is about two hours away. When she got there,
the pre-counselling session was just a judgemental session. Healthcare
workers imposing their beliefs on her. Telling her she shouldn't abort.
They started telling her about God. She left without doing the abortion.
— Onke Jezile[1]

These are the words of Onke Jezile, founder of Lethabo la Azania,
a non-profit organisation that works with children and the youth
in Engcobo, a village in the Eastern Cape. Jezile says the pregnant
(cisgender) woman referred to above eventually went to Marie Stopes, a
private, non-profit provider of reproductive and health services, in East
London, three hours away by car from Engcobo. When she arrived, the
clinic was already closing for the day. She was told to return the next day,
something she could not afford.[2]

This book is about these kinds of pregnant people who live in rural
areas in the Eastern Cape province of South Africa and face multiple
challenges in accessing abortion services, even when the abortion they
seek is legal. Through in-depth mixed-methods research, we highlight
the complex and interlinked challenges community members point to in
navigating the uncertain path of deciding on an abortion and accessing

abortion services, as well as their expressed preferences regarding these services. Throughout the book, we note that there are no quick or easy answers to providing stigma-free, accessible, acceptable and affordable abortion services in South Africa's rural areas. It is clear, however, that these services are not readily accessible for various reasons. In brief, this book scrutinises the possibilities of ensuring that pregnant people in rural areas are not denied their rights regarding a fundamental repro-ductive healthcare service – abortion.

WHY STUDY ACCESS TO ABORTION, AND WHY IN RURAL AREAS?

Access to abortion services varies considerably across the globe. One of the most significant factors influencing access is, of course, legislation. At the time of writing, 24 countries (out of 195 worldwide, or just under one in eight) banned abortion in all circumstances. Most countries, however, grant abortion under particular circumstances, some very restrictive, some more liberal. Where abortion is allowed on request, there may be a time limit (often up to 12 weeks of gestation – the first trimester of preg-nancy). Where abortion is not allowed on request, grounds for granting abortion tend to include some or all the following: cases of rape, incest, risk to the life or health of the pregnant person, impairment of the foetus and severe socio-economic hardship. Legislation may also speak to such matters as parental consent in the case of minors; spousal consent in the case of married people; police reports in the case of rape; restricting access to methods to determine the sex of the foetus (this is mainly the case where sex-selective abortion – usually of female foetuses – is practised); mandatory or non-mandatory counselling; waiting time; and requiring the pregnant person to first view an ultrasound or listen for a foetal heartbeat before receiving an abortion.

South Africa, where this research was conducted, has liberal abortion laws. The Choice on Termination of Pregnancy Act (henceforth CTOP Act) and other health legislation[3] changed the country's landscape of reproductive health to align with the post-apartheid government's commitment to reproductive health rights.[4] The decision to abort a pregnancy within the first 12 weeks of gestation is placed with the pregnant person. All pregnant people, including minors, may request an abortion in the first trimester of pregnancy. The grounds for medical practitioners to grant an abortion in later stages of pregnancy are relatively open (including the socio-economic effects on the pregnant person of continuing the pregnancy).

The CTOP Act indicates that 'the State has the responsibility to provide reproductive health to all, and also to provide safe conditions under which the right of choice can be exercised'.[5] Up to 12 weeks of gestation, professional midwives and registered nurses can provide an abortion, and the service can be performed at primary-care health facilities. A 2008 amendment[6] allows any health facility with a 24-hour maternity service to offer first-trimester abortion services without the ministerial permission that was previously required.

Despite the promise of the CTOP Act and initial indications of its implementation leading to decreased maternal morbidity and mortality, several challenges have been noted.[7] These include:

1. staff at referral centres dissuading women from seeking abortions[8] (referred to in the opening epigraph of this chapter);
2. health service providers and facility managers citing conscientious objection to providing services;[9]
3. many designated facilities are not functioning;[10]
4. women not receiving the abortions that they requested;[11]
5. women seeking care outside of their residential area for fear of breaches of confidentiality;[12]
6. the stigma associated with abortion, particularly for HIV-positive women;[13] and
7. lack of state-led information campaigns resulting in pregnant women not knowing their rights under the CTOP Act.[14]

Because of poor or inaccessible legal services, many pregnant people continue to procure abortions from traditional healers,[15] from health professionals performing abortions without Department of Health designation,[16] or by using herbal infusions to self-abort.[17] These are illegal abortions, many of which will be unsafe.[18]

The causes of this lacklustre service provision are multiple. Cathi Albertyn argues that the initial advances after the promulgation of CTOP Act have been pushed back because of a declining health system, the pervasive stigma surrounding abortion, healthcare provider resistance, a reduced non-governmental sector and unclear political will.[19] Crucially, the consequences of these challenges are not felt equally across the South African population. Indeed, poor black (cis)women and (cis)women living in rural areas are more likely to die from abortion-related complications than their urban, white and wealthier counterparts.[20] Poor black (cis)women in rural areas face the same barriers as other black (cis)women (negative healthcare worker attitudes, a failing health system, fears around confidentiality, and so on). In addition, however, access to abortion services by rural people is hampered by the long distances to facilities and high transport costs – again, something noted by Onke in the opening epigraph.[21]

With these issues in mind, we focus in this book on location, particularly on uneven access to abortion services for populations living in rural areas. We explore the possibilities and challenges of providing abortion care in low-income rural areas with limited access to healthcare facilities and where social norms and knowledge of abortion care may present barriers to women's ability to seek an abortion. The study was conducted in partnership with Marie Stopes South Africa (MSSA). Our research aimed to assist MSSA in focusing their service delivery on overcoming barriers to safe abortion care, reducing stigma and ensuring access to appropriate service provision for the rural populations of the Eastern Cape. The report provided to MSSA, different from this book, may be found on the website of the Critical Studies in Sexualities and Reproduction research programme at Rhodes University.[22]

A BRIEF HISTORY OF ABORTION AND REPRODUCTIVE CONTROL IN SOUTH AFRICA

As is the case on all other continents, abortion has been practised in Africa, including the southern tip of Africa, throughout history.[23] Abortion in South Africa has been the subject of several excellent historical studies that situate its practice and regulation within the social and political context of the country and the time, covering traditional and medical practices through to the regulation of abortion and, finally, the liberalisation of abortion laws in 1996.[24]

In the nineteenth century and the first part of the twentieth century, South Africa was governed by a mixture of common laws inherited from its colonists. These laws were mostly traditionalist and illiberal, in line with colonial and nineteenth-century thinking. For example, abortion was illegal under common law inherited from England, allowed only in cases where the pregnant woman's life was at risk.

With the advent of apartheid (1948–1994), various sexual and reproductive control measures were legislated in civil law in line with Dutch Reformed Calvinist and Afrikaner nationalist ideologies.[25] These included the 1949 Prohibition of Mixed Marriages Act[26] and the 1950 Immorality Amendment Act,[27] which criminalised marriage and extramarital sex between 'Europeans' and people of other races, and nullified any such existing marriages. To enforce these laws and other race-based legislation, the Population Registration Act was passed in 1950, requiring all South Africans to register their race based on their physical appearance and linguistic skills.[28] The 1969 Immorality Amendment Act[29] criminalised homosexuality and anything related to 'unnatural' sexual acts, including the sale of sex toys, although homosexual acts had been prohibited by the inherited Roman-Dutch law before that.

It was within these reproductive regulatory controls that questions around abortion arose. Until 1975, the common law regarding abortion was not heavily enforced. In the early 1970s, various hospitals across the country revealed the extent of clandestine abortion, complaining that abortion-related cases were using up their gynaecological budgets.[30] This provided the impetus for abortion to become a public debate.[31] In her book on abortion under apartheid, Susanne Klausen relates how South African women were aborting pregnancies at home or with informal providers and then using the hospital as a backup to ensure they did not die.

> Hospitals reported a spike in patients on Fridays: women clearly planned to have their abortions on weekends so they could return to school or work on Mondays. In 1974, Baragwanath [Hospital] set up two wards every weekend just to accommodate abortion cases. Clearly, women saw hospitals as a crucial resource to be utilized when necessary.[32]

The majority of the women arriving at hospitals seeking care after abortions were black; consequently, the issue was not high on the apartheid government's agenda. Instead the government attempted to cover up the alarming statistics.[33] The apartheid authorities wished only to stop white women from procuring abortions.[34] However, the government could no longer ignore the issue of illegal abortions when, during the early 1970s, there were several high-profile cases of white women, especially teenagers, procuring abortions.[35]

In 1975, the Abortion and Sterilization Act[36] was passed. This Act broadened the scope of legal abortion from being provided only when there was a threat to the pregnant woman's life to allowing abortion in cases of severe foetal abnormality, rape and incest, and where a pregnant woman was deemed 'mentally incompetent'. The process of gaining permission to have the abortion was extensive, however, requiring the consent at least three doctors.[37] The Act put renewed focus on targeting and prosecuting illegal abortionists. Clandestine abortions continued, however, with very few women obtaining permission to have a legal abortion.[38]

The fight for abortion rights in South Africa during apartheid was led by the medical profession rather than by feminists, which, as Klausen notes, is more in line with the story of the United States than of Europe.[39] Regardless, this fight was largely fruitless and only democracy would bring around the opportunity for reform. As Rebecca Hodes shows, the post-apartheid liberalisation of abortion laws was not uncontested.[40] Nonetheless, the CTOP Act was passed thanks to the African National Congress (ANC) executive branch ensuring a parliamentary majority by rejecting calls for an 'open vote', which would have allowed parliamentarians to vote as individuals. An open vote would have most likely ensured the rejection of the CTOP Act since there was (and still is) significant opposition to abortion within the ANC and across the country.[41] Knowledge of the health consequences of illegal abortions, especially the fact that most people who die from these are black, played an important role in the passage of the CTOP Act and its continued approval.

The CTOP Act, which took effect in February 1997, has been hailed as a progressive law. The sole rigidity in the Act is that only medical doctors and registered nurses can administer abortion pills in the first trimester. This rules out the possibility of pharmacies dispensing mifepristone and misoprostol, which research has shown to be 'effective and acceptable to patients, with a low prevalence of adverse events'.[42] Surgical abortions (vacuum aspiration or dilation and curettage) are only allowed to be administered by medical doctors, which means they are not available in primary-level clinics mainly staffed by nurses. This is problematic since the hospitals where second-trimester abortions are allowed are concentrated in urban centres.[43]

RURALITY: ITS MEANINGS AND COMPLICATIONS

The term 'rural' is often used as a self-evident signifier. It is the opposite of 'urban'; it suggests wider spaces, lower population densities, and different work-related and leisure activities in relation to the 'urban'. And yet, on closer inspection, there is a slipperiness around the boundaries between rural and urban and a lack of a clear, agreed-upon definition. Two other complications arise. First, while 'rural' is often used to demarcate geographical areas, it is also used in sociocultural ways. Second, significant variations exist *within* each broad 'urban' and 'rural' category. We discuss these complications below.

Government definitions of rurality are often based on population metrics, particularly density. Areas with high population densities are 'urban', and those with low densities are 'rural'. Some countries, however, designate areas by sectoral employment (e.g., areas where most people are employed in the agricultural sector are classified as rural) or by provision of infrastructure and services in the area. Unfortunately, definitions of rural areas differ significantly from one country to another, which makes it difficult to compare these areas across national borders.[44] This, of course, has implications for our research findings in terms of its applicability outside of the South African context.

In addition, definitions of urban and rural are complicated by the legacy of apartheid in South Africa. Commercial farmlands in the areas previously demarcated for white people during apartheid are classified as rural, along with areas under the jurisdiction of traditional authorities (or traditional chiefs) in previous 'homelands' – areas designated for limited self-government by black people during apartheid. The latter areas are considered rural mainly due to their lack of infrastructure (a legacy of apartheid exclusions) rather than population density.[45]

These two broad categories of 'rural' (commercial farmlands and traditional authority areas) differ regarding several variables. A fundamental difference is landownership. Commercial farms are owned by individuals, corporations or, with the institution of land reform post-apartheid, community trusts. Farm labourers form a high proportion of residents in these areas. 'Traditional' areas have communal land tenure. In these cases, the government owns the land but manages it through tribal authorities. This occurs mainly in the former homelands, two of which are situated in the Eastern Cape where we conducted our research – the former Ciskei and the former Transkei. As outlined by Michael Clark and Nolundi Luwaya:

> The legal insecurity of land tenure is a critical challenge facing those living in communal areas. In many areas individuals or families that have occupied and used the same piece of land undisturbed for generations may find that they have weak legal claims to the land they inhabit.[46]

There are other ways in which the two categories differ. For example, as outlined by Sharthi Laldaparsad, commercial farmland households tend to use gas, paraffin, wood or coal as the primary energy source for cooking, while those in communal land tenure areas use animal dung or solar. Water tends to be supplied by boreholes in the former, while rivers and springs are often relied on in the latter.[47]

As detailed below in the discussion of our research methodology, we purposefully accessed three rural sites based on diversity within the notion of 'rural' in the Eastern Cape context. Two sites are in former homeland areas – one very remote and one more accessible. One of the sites is in a commercial farmland area.

Since the demise of apartheid and its strict laws on the movement of black people, South Africa has seen growing urbanisation. The percentage of the population classified as rural decreased between censuses: from 45% in 1996 to 43% in 2001 and 37% in 2011.[48] This trend results in resources being focused on urban areas. Resource constraints, however, are not felt evenly in rural areas. As noted by Johannes Tsheola, many rural people live 'within tribal settlements of the former Bantustans wherein colonialism and apartheid destroyed the asset base and reinforced a strong correlation between poverty and gender'.[49] On commercial farmlands, farm owners and corporate managers live in relative prosperity, while farm workers live on low wages, are generally not unionised and sometimes face evictions. Women workers bear the brunt of the casualisation of labour, are generally paid less than men and often have no independent right to tenure or housing.[50]

While 'rural' has geographical connotations, it also has sociocultural meanings. Rural areas may be seen as land spaces that enable culturally defined identities, which include having a rural background even if one is living in an urban area. Community bonds and traditionalism are often seen as defining rural areas, although researchers emphasise the hetero-geneous and context-dependent nature of rurality.[51] While our research concentrates on geographical location, specifically three diverse rural sites, we asked participants to provide input on community responses and actions. In this way, we tap into contextual community narratives and social practices – in a sense, rural sociocultural responses to abortion and abortion services.

SITE SAMPLING

We conducted our research in 2019–2020 in the Eastern Cape, a large province formed from two former homelands (Ciskei and Transkei) and the eastern section of the former Cape province. At the time of writing, the Eastern Cape was the poorest province in the country, par-tially because of the legacy of apartheid that saw homeland areas being underdeveloped and forming labour reserves for the large mining corporations.[52] The black African population group (from which we drew our entire sample) is the largest in the province (6.1 million of 6.8 million inhabitants).[53]

To capture the diversity of the rurality of the Eastern Cape, three sites, shown in figure 0.1, were selected based on the Municipal Demarcation Board's classifications: the B3 category comprises local municipalities with small towns but with no large town as the core; the B4 category is made up of local municipalities that are mainly rural with communal tenure and with, at most, one or two small towns. We partnered with a non-governmental organisation (NGO) in each site that has established roots in the area.

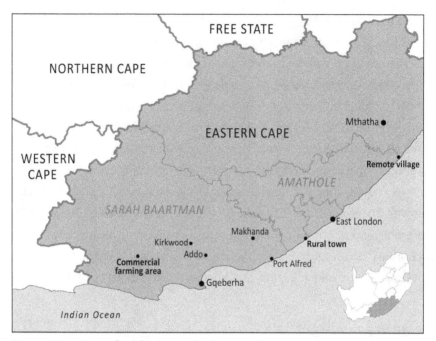

Figure 0.1: Map of study sites in the Eastern Cape

The site we call the 'commercial farming area' is a B3 local municipality in the Sarah Baartman district municipality. We included this
site to cover commercial farm workers. The research site was selected
with the help of our partner NGO, the East Cape Agricultural Research
Project (ECARP), which operates across the western part of the province where most commercial farming takes place (see figure 0.1).[54] In
this area, clinics are not easily accessible since they are situated mainly in
towns. A mobile clinic services most citizens living on farms. The clinic
consists of a pickup truck with its canopy converted into a mini clinic.

The other two sites fall under B4 local municipalities. The site we will
call the 'rural town' is a sizeable rural zone surrounding a small town in the
western part of the Amathole district municipality. The area was previously
part of Ciskei. At the time of the study, an estimated 2 000 people lived
around the town. There is a clinic in town and a hospital in a neighbouring
town. The local NGO, Keiskamma Trust, provides basic health services

through its home-based carers, among a variety of other services.[55] Our third site, the 'remote village', consists of four villages on the eastern side of the Amathole district municipality. This area was previously part of the Transkei. An estimated 6 000 people live in these four villages. The local NGO Bulungula Incubator provides most of the healthcare and other services in the area.[56] Besides Bulungula Incubator's health point in one of the villages (which employs a nurse and provides basic primary healthcare services), there were no health services in the area at the time of our study. There are two clinics in neighbouring villages and two hospitals in distant towns. The Keiskamma Trust and Bulungula Incubator home-based carers were pivotal in our data-collection process, and their health programme coordinators, Nomthandazo Manjezi and Bongezwa Sontuntu, respectively, provided valuable input as part of our study's expert panel.

OUR RESEARCH

We applied a social scientific, mixed-methods approach in our research. A qualitative component consisting of individual community informant interviews formed the first component of the study. This was followed by a quantitative discrete choice experiment (DCE). A literature review and a qualitative study formed the foundation of the DCE.

Qualitative component

Given the sensitive nature of reproductive health issues, including abortion, individual rather than focus group interviews were conducted with 60 people (20 from each site). Purposive sampling was employed for the qualitative data collection. Participants were selected to fit the purpose of potentially needing reproductive health and abortion services in the area. That is, they needed to be (1) of reproductive age (between 18 and 45 years old), and (2) a permanent resident of the area. In each site, the NGO partner identified and approached 20 participants based on the selection criteria. Of the 20 participants in each site, two were men.

A pilot study was conducted to test the draft interview guide once ethics clearance was obtained from the Rhodes University Ethical Standards Committee and the Marie Stopes International Independent Ethics in Research Committee. This consisted of four interviews in the rural town. Information from the pilot study fed back into the review of the instrument as well as the training of fieldworkers. The interview guide and consent forms were translated into isiXhosa through a rigorous back-translation process.

Participants were treated as community informants, reflecting not only on their understandings but also on those of the community within which they live. A decision was taken not to specifically recruit participants who had undergone an abortion, although they were not excluded. (As there are no abortion clinics close to the areas in which we conducted the research, we could not recruit participants in such clinics.) In addition, given the intimate nature of many rural communities (certainly in the remote village and the rural town) and the possibility of abortion stigma, we considered it ethically unsuitable to make, at the outset, having had an abortion a requirement for participation. As such, our research taps into community understandings rather than individual experiences (although some participants also spoke about personal experiences).

The duration of interviews varied but these were mostly between 30 minutes and an hour long. Interview questions elicited data on participants' reports of their community's understanding of problematic/unwanted pregnancies, abortion, abortion legislation and abortion services; the barriers to, and facilitators of, access to abortion services; perceptions of safety and quality of current abortion services; and recommendations for new or improved services. Participants were given the option of being interviewed at their home or at a neutral space such as a local NGO office, which, in each site, was hired for the occasion.

The fieldworkers for the qualitative phase were drawn from the Rhodes University postgraduate student population and were thoroughly trained. Each fieldworker completed an online ethics course before the commencement of training and signed a confidentiality agreement.

Interviews were conducted in participants' preferred language (isiXhosa or English) and were audio-recorded with participants' permission.

Transcription and translation of the interviews by researchers fluent in English and isiXhosa occurred after the fieldwork. These data were analysed using interpretive content analysis.[57] Interpretive content analysis enables an understanding of specified characteristics and categories of data, refined and revised in an analytical feedback loop. In this process, both manifest content (characteristics that are readily identifiable in the data) and latent content (characteristics that are not overtly evident but are implicit or implied across the data) are analysed. An example of the latent content of our data is the key problematic identified in this study: the conundrum of confidentiality versus cost.

Quantitative component

The quantitative part of the research consisted of a discrete choice experiment (DCE) conducted in each of the three sites. The DCE design has been used in several areas, including consumer products, customer services and healthcare services. This methodology allows researchers to investigate how people in a particular context rate selected attributes of a service by asking them to state their preference for different hypothetical alternatives.[58] Each alternative is described by attributes, and responses are used to infer the value placed on each attribute. This approach allows for the calculation of participants' trade-offs between attributes. The technique is useful where there is an intention to extend or alter services (or provide new ones where services do not yet exist).

Figure 0.2 outlines the steps in conducting the DCE. Themes from the qualitative component and our literature review formed the basis for designing the questionnaire, in line with the ISPOR Task Force's suggestions for good research practices regarding conjoint analysis, which includes DCEs.[59]

The question that the DCE answered was, 'What are people's preferences for facility, location, provider type, information channels and costs when

Figure 0.2: Research steps in the DCE

hypothetically accessing abortion services in the Eastern Cape?' The following aspects were identified as potential attributes from the literature review, qualitative data, input from an expert panel (consisting of representatives of the NGOs, MSSA and the research team) and researcher discussions: facility type, additional services offered, abortion type, travelling distance, abortion cost and opening times. Levels were decided upon for each of these attributes. These can be viewed in figure 0.3, which contains an example of one (of ten) of our choice tasks. Participants were asked to point out which one of the three options they were most likely to choose.

For the study, the DCE had ten choice tasks with six attributes of between three and six levels. This aligns with trends concerning the

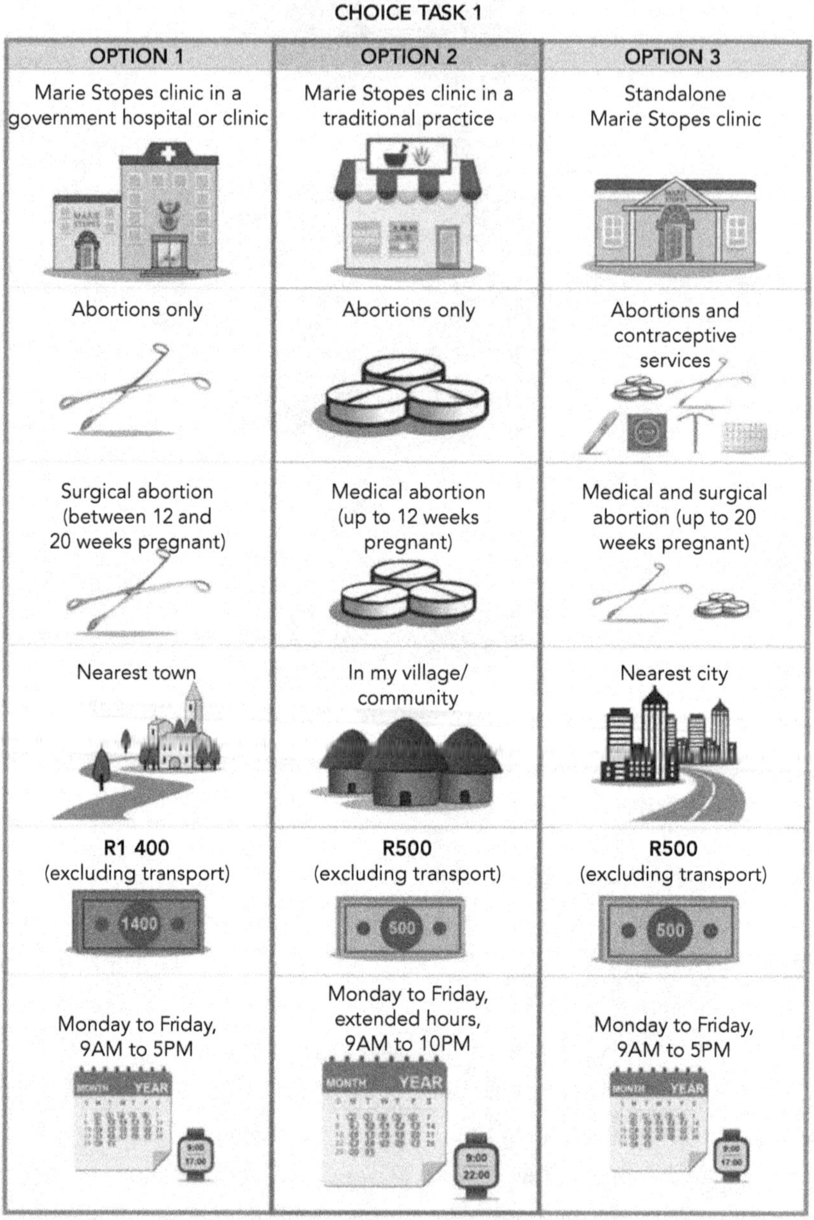

CHOICE TASK 1

OPTION 1	OPTION 2	OPTION 3
Marie Stopes clinic in a government hospital or clinic	Marie Stopes clinic in a traditional practice	Standalone Marie Stopes clinic
Abortions only	Abortions only	Abortions and contraceptive services
Surgical abortion (between 12 and 20 weeks pregnant)	Medical abortion (up to 12 weeks pregnant)	Medical and surgical abortion (up to 20 weeks pregnant)
Nearest town	In my village/ community	Nearest city
R1 400 (excluding transport)	**R500** (excluding transport)	**R500** (excluding transport)
Monday to Friday, 9AM to 5PM	Monday to Friday, extended hours, 9AM to 10PM	Monday to Friday, 9AM to 5PM

Figure 0.3:   Example of a choice task

number of choice tasks and attributes, with fewer tasks resulting in an instrument that is less burdensome to complete. Given that the current

Table 0.1: Demographic characteristics of the DCE sample

Variable	n	Estimate (%)	CI 95%	Missing (n)
Sex				8
Female	496	82	(78, 85)	
Male	112	18	(15, 22)	
Site				
Remote village	207	34	(30, 37)	
Rural town	209	34	(30, 38)	
Commercial farming area	200	32	(29, 36)	
... in rural area				6
Live ...	421	69	(65, 73)	
Live and work ...	130	21	(18, 25)	
Work ...	21	3	(2, 5)	
None	38	6	(4, 8)	
Employed				7
Yes	144	24	(20, 27)	
No	465	76	(73, 80)	
Income				26
R0–1 000	328	56	(52, 60)	
R1 000–2 000	179	30	(27, 34)	
R2 000–5 000	63	11	(8, 13)	
R5 000+	20	3	(2, 5)	

study was conducted among participants from rural communities with lower access to formal education,[60] and in line with other studies conducted in low-resource, marginalised communities, pictorial representations were incorporated to contribute to the instrument's usability. The understandability and effectiveness of the pictorial representations and the DCE exercise were assessed during pilot testing.

Our sample consisted of 616 participants. The demographic and socio-economic characteristics of the sampled participants are shown in table 0.1. More than 80% of the final sample were women (n = 496), while approximately 18% were men (n = 112). The average age at the time of data collection was 29.3 years old (CI = 28.7, 30.0), and no statistically significant differences were observed in the average age between male and female participants (28.1 versus 29.6 years old for men and women respectively; p = 0.142). At the time of data collection, all the participants lived in the selected sites. Only a quarter of the sample was employed, with no statistically significant differences in employment status between men and women. Monthly income was relatively low, with more than half of the participants (56%) reporting a monthly income of R0–1 000 and only 3% earning more than R5 000 per month.

The quantitative data analysis was conducted by a statistician and consisted of descriptive and inferential analysis, including regression models. Regression analysis allowed an assessment of the participants' preferences for a specific attribute level as well as the strength of their preferences. Details of quality assurance and ethical considerations can be viewed in the report provided to MSSA.[61]

OVERVIEW OF CHAPTERS

The chapters that follow build on one another. Accurate knowledge of basic issues regarding abortion is fundamental to accessing services. We therefore start by outlining the participants' reported knowledge of abortion legislation, facilities and procedures, as well as their information sources (chapter 1). We then discuss participants' renditions of the abortion decision-making process (chapter 2). We outline participants' input regarding partner-related and family-related dynamics. Unsurprisingly, given the locations where the research was conducted, the issue of poverty arose in relation to abortion decision making and the lack of quality antenatal care.

In chapter 3, we outline participants' renditions of community attitudes and understandings of abortion. We discuss anti-abortion sentiments based on moral or damage stories. While these kinds of attitudes were said to be widespread, there was also an acknowledgement that abortion is a disputed issue and an indication that abortion is acceptable in the case of rape. Pregnancy among teenagers was viewed as problematic and as leading to abortion.

We build on chapter 3 to discuss a key issue that arose in our data – stigma – in chapter 4. Initially, our study did not focus on abortion stigma per se; instead, we aimed to investigate attitudes towards and preferences for abortion services. However, even the most basic reading of our data showed quite clearly that the effects of stigma attached to abortion are perhaps the most detrimental to the realisation of the right to access a safe abortion in these rural areas. In this chapter, we outline a conceptual framework for stigma, then outline reported experienced, perceived and internalised stigma as well as accounts of stigma management.

In chapter 5, we discuss findings in relation to barriers to abortion services. These include breaches of confidentiality, distance and costs, fear of abortion consequences, hostility from health service providers and partner dynamics. In chapter 6, we discuss the results of the DCE regarding preferences for type of abortion facilities, the location of facilities, the services offered, costs, opening time and information channels.

The findings of this study are brought together in the concluding chapter. We use a reproductive justice approach to analyse the implications of the findings. Reproductive justice is an approach developed by women of colour in North America[62] and fleshed out by scholars in the global South.[63] The approach combines rights-based arguments with the principles of social justice. This chapter addresses the central conundrum underpinning abortion services in these rural areas: confidentiality versus cost.

1

'If it is Legal These Days, I Do Not Know': Knowledge of Abortion Legislation and Services

The CTOP Act was promulgated to ensure that all pregnant people have the power to decide the outcome of a pregnancy, whether it be abortion, taking the pregnancy to term, adoption or keeping the infant. For this to be a reality, however, accurate knowledge about available choices, including abortion, is necessary. Of course, such knowledge is a necessary, but not sufficient, condition for accessing legal abortion services. Various other barriers may obstruct access; these are dealt with in the following chapters.

Awareness of the legal status of abortion is one component of knowledge about abortion. A review of global research on young people's knowledge of abortion found that while young people may have knowledge of abortion in general, they lack specific knowledge.[1] Knowledge of the various stipulations of the relevant laws, where to access abortion and what to expect when requesting an abortion are all important. In this chapter, we outline findings from the qualitative component of our research: participants' input on their own and their community's knowledge of abortion laws, abortion facilities, abortion procedures and sources of information. We supplement our analysis with results from quantitative South African studies on abortion knowledge. While quantitative studies provide information on the extent of the knowledge, our qualitative data point to various dynamics within the circulation of knowledge in the rural areas we studied.

KNOWLEDGE OF ABORTION LAWS

Knowledge about the CTOP Act was first investigated in the 1998 South African Demographic and Health Survey (SADHS), soon after the passing of the Act. At that time it was found that only 53% of women knew about the law and that a pregnancy could be terminated legally during the first 12 weeks of gestation.[2] Knowledge was poorest among teenagers, women living in rural areas, those with less education and black women, especially those aged 45–49. Unfortunately, later Demographic and Health Surveys did not include this question. Following the 1998 SADHS, a study was conducted in the Western Cape of women presenting at 26 public health clinics in an urban and a rural health district.[3] Thirty-two per cent of the women did not know that abortion is legal in South Africa, with women presenting at rural clinics being significantly more likely not to know the legal status of abortion than those at urban clinics. At about the same time, Kelvin Mwaba and Pamela Naidoo surveyed undergraduate psychology students from a South African university, a population that would be expected to be relatively well informed.[4] The results showed that 19% of male and 16% of female students believed that abortion was illegal in South Africa. Two more recent studies explored high school learners' knowledge – one conducted in the Eastern Cape[5] and one in KwaZulu-Natal.[6] In the former study, 47% of respondents were aware of the legal status of abortion, while in the latter, the percentage was 80%.

Knowledge of the various legal stipulations was poor in both studies, however. For example, in the Eastern Cape study, only 25.1% knew that parental consent was not required for a minor to terminate a pregnancy. In the KwaZulu-Natal study, only 6.7% knew this stipulation.

Much like the research showed, our impression from our interviews was that there was reasonably widespread basic knowledge of the legality of abortion among our participants, but they were hazy on the details. In addition, most participants could identify which type of abortion service provider was legal and which was not.

> It is legal because it is now being talked about in the news and in the papers that doing an abortion is legal. (Andisiwe, rural town)[7]
>
> Because you might buy someone to help you abort illegally. That is not right by the law. Someone will offer money and ask for a fast way of abortion, and that is not right, you have to follow the rules of the law to get to where you want. (Athule, commercial farming area)
>
> That which is unlawful, sister, is the one written on papers where a person will write and say they can perform an abortion and leave their number. You cannot trust that one. Rather go to a doctor. (Nasipi, commercial farming area)
>
> The illegal way of doing an abortion is doing it yourself by just drinking something. The legal way is going to the clinic. (Gcobisa, remote village)

In these extracts, legal abortion is contrasted with illegal abortion, which participants refer to as 'doing it yourself' (self-induction) and procuring an abortion from an informal provider. Illegal abortion providers are negatively portrayed, as they are deemed not to be trusted.

Some participants believed that abortion was illegal or reported that their community members might believe it was illegal.

> They do as they please, but the law does not state that it is lawful. (Khunjulwa, remote village)

No, that has never been legal. Well, we don't know it is as legal as the olden-day people. If it is legal these days, I do not know. (Mafungwashe, remote village)

She can hide it because it is said that it is legal, but not really … not really. (Amanda, rural town)

Others know, but there aren't many people who know, and others simply just do not care. (Thulani, commercial farming area)

I think … yes, we do know that we have a right to terminate pregnancy. Is that correct? … but I think older people don't know that. We, young people, know that. (Khethiwe, remote village)

Here some participants state outright that abortion is not legal, while others prevaricate – perhaps it is legal or perhaps it is not. Lack of knowledge is attributed to not caring or to age (with older people being positioned as less knowledgeable than younger people). Given the restrictive nature of abortion legislation in South Africa before the CTOP Act, such responses, especially from older people, are unsurprising.

Some participants thought that abortion was illegal and that it should be legalised.

I would say it should be made legal because we live in a time where people are being raped. We live in a time where women are raped on the streets. Sometimes women are raped at home by a relative. Children are raped at a young age maybe by their uncles and would be quiet about it until the family notices that they are pregnant. (Athenkosi, commercial farming area)

In this extract, the belief that abortion is illegal is accompanied by an argument for its legalisation because of the high incidence of rape. This dovetails with the notion of abortion being conditionally acceptable – that is, only under particular circumstances (in this case, rape). This line of thinking is explored further in chapter 3.

In contrast, several participants knew that abortion is legal but believed that it should not be or reported that their community members did not support it being legal.

> People understand that the abortion law in South Africa is not welcome because it is written in the Bible; it says increase family members; it does not want abortion, but the South African law allows for abortion. (Siphamandla, rural town)
>
> In my opinion, it is legal only according to government laws. But in my opinion, I view it as an illegal practice. (Simbongile, rural town)
>
> Yes, even though they may know abortion laws, they will never consider it as legal. They know what is wrong and right. (Ziyanda, commercial farming area)

Participants draw a distinction here between the legal and moral status of abortion. Drawing from religious metaphors, participants differentiate between the law and what is 'right'. The extracts presented thus far reflect the varied attitudes towards the legal status of abortion in these communities.

Research has revealed a number of misconceptions concerning the various stipulations of the CTOP Act. For example, in a study by Devashnee Ramiyad and Cynthia Patel, which explored South African adolescents' knowledge of abortion legislation and attitudes in KwaZulu-Natal, participants showed limited knowledge of specific aspects of the Act: only 10.7% were aware of the period of gestation when termination is permitted on request; 28.7% knew who is allowed to perform the procedure; and 29.3% were aware that it is a criminal offence to prevent or obstruct access to a legal abortion.[8] This lack of specific knowledge is confirmed in a study on knowledge among high school learners in the Eastern Cape.[9]

Similarly, in our study, some participants indicated that while community members did know that abortion is legal, many did not understand the nuances of the legislation.

> They know the laws created by the government, but they still need help because they do not know [understand] them fully. (Kuhle, remote village)
>
> To be honest, the youth is very knowledgeable about abortion, but 50% of them do not know the relevant information. They do not know that they have the right to have an abortion and that no one can say no, and that it is actually legal for them to terminate a pregnancy. It would be ideal if someone could give them full information about where they can go and other options, to inform them that it is their right and it is legal. (Ntobeko, rural town)

Here age is once again mentioned as a factor in knowledge, except young people are now singled out. Ntobeko's assertion that 'no one can say no' refers to the misconception, also revealed in the research referred to above, that parental or guardian permission is required for minors to terminate a pregnancy.

Besides reporting on flawed specific knowledge among community members, participants themselves had some misconceptions. Three months of pregnancy was often given as the cut-off date for a legal abortion, but sometimes an earlier date or stage was cited ('before the bones are formed' [Esona, rural town]).

> They do the abortion process if you're at least two months pregnant. If you are three months, they can't. (Lulama, remote village)
>
> I know the one that says you can't abort if you have been pregnant for more than three months. I don't know any other law besides that. You can tell me. (Khethiwe, remote village)
>
> Therefore, you need to have three months or below. Even if you are three months with two days extra, you cannot because now the baby is developing, and it is starting to be more like a person as it is developing. So, if you are three months or less, you can get an abortion, but if you have an abortion after the three-month period,

you will be at risk of losing your life. You can get it done, but you might also die right away. (Bulelani, rural town)

While some of this information is accurate (up to 12 weeks gestation, abortion is legal on request), there are also some inaccuracies. First, abortion can be performed after three months of pregnancy under particular conditions, including for socio-economic reasons. Second, abortion in the second trimester, if conducted safely, is unlikely to cause death. The reported inaccuracies may be related to the fact that second-trimester abortions are performed in very few facilities, most of which are located in urban areas. Stories abound of the challenges women face in accessing such abortions.[10] These can easily translate into local narratives of second-trimester abortions being illegal or highly dangerous.

KNOWLEDGE OF ABORTION FACILITIES

Knowledge of the existence of abortion facilities was reportedly wide-spread. Participants indicated that most people know to go to clinics, hospitals or private doctors either to procure an abortion or to receive the correct information.

> No, there is no other option except going to the hospital. (Akhona, remote village)
> She can go to the clinic. She can go to the hospital or to a private doctor if she has the money. If she can afford it. In that place, in government, that can provide appropriate care for someone … There are other places, but you find that they are not legal … So, the best place you can go is government places, clinics, public clinics. (Amahle, rural town)

Here participants refer to legal service providers – government or private practitioners. Amahle also refers to illegal providers. Indeed, illegal providers have proliferated, taking advantage of an environment in which

Figure 1.1: Abortion advert posted on a street in the Eastern Cape (photo courtesy of Megan Reuvers)

people lack knowledge of legal providers, cannot access these providers or fear breaches of confidentiality in government clinics (we discuss this further in chapter 4). Although Amahle refers to illegal abortion providers, they were reported to be unavailable in the communities that formed part of the study. Instead, they were said to be available only in cities or large towns. Indeed, most urban spaces are festooned with illegal adverts offering abortions (ironically, often paired with penis enlargements, as shown in figure 1.1), especially along transport routes.

Knowledge of facilities that provide legal services was not the same as knowing where they are located.

> What I can say is that we hear that there is a place that conducts abortions for a person who does not want her pregnancy, even though we do not know where these places are located. (Anathi, remote village)

> There's a place for abortion at [closest city]. Apparently, there's another one here in [this area], but I don't know where it is. (Esihle, remote village)

For women to access an abortion, knowledge of the legal status of abortion and that legal abortion providers exist must be supplemented with knowledge of the location of services. Indeed, it can often be difficult for abortion seekers to ascertain where clinics are. Bhekisisa, an investigative health journalism centre, took up this issue. They published a list of functioning government clinics because there 'was no such database available for the public'. However, on their first attempt, the list was outdated before it was even published. They explained that this was 'because termination of pregnancy services are fragile. Very often, they depend upon a single midwife at a facility who is willing to do the job. When that staff member leaves, the service disappears.'[11] The non-profit organisation Triad Trust is now maintaining the list. The map of facilities is called 'Where to Care'.[12] However, many people living in rural areas with limited access to the internet or data will be unable to search and find this site or other information.

Participants indicated that traditional healers who provide abortions are not widespread. Regardless, traditional healers were seen as not providing safe abortions.

> The traditional ways are available, but not in this community. Even those that use such things, they go to the township at [an area some distance away]. (Ziyanda, commercial farming area)
>
> We end up knowing those who secretly went to have an abortion the traditional way, and they also end up being a burden when there are complications, having to be taken to hospitals … I can just say we do need to have abortions here in this community, but not the traditional one because it is not right. The clinical one is the right one because they do it effectively, and your safety is ensured. I support it. (Khethiwe, remote village)

Here traditional healers are viewed as providing abortions in which the pregnant woman's safety is jeopardised, leading to complications.

Some participants spoke of common knowledge concerning self-abortion using local abortifacients (substances used to induce an abortion).

> So in the case that I do not have money to go to [the city] to get an abortion, my friend will come along and give me a plan. I'll tell her, 'Friend so-and-so got me pregnant, but I do not want a child.' She'll say, 'Don't worry, this is easy. I'll make you a mixture of plants and herbs.' (Fezeka, remote village)

> Yes, others abort by themselves in their houses. They also know herbs from the forest; they, therefore, drink those to abort … We recommend places for each other. For instance, you recommend the one you once went to. (Esihle, remote village)

> She had already drunk [methylated] spirits and Disprin tablets. She said she had tried everything that we usually talked about, even raw Oro Crush, but nothing helped. (Thato, rural town)

> Maybe it's the money, and she does not have it, I don't know. Because I don't know how much abortion is. Oro Crush was inexpensive, hence it was popular back in the day. Then a woman would buy R50 pills to clean her womb. (Thembeka, remote village)

> Hey, no, I have not heard of any challenges. I just heard about the Oro Crush juice and steel wool being used for abortions [laughs] How these are used, I do not know, and I am not sure if that is the truth. (Noludwe, remote village)

> … someone drank uMadubula, [household disinfectant] and the other one remained having a baby. (Lithalethu, rural town)

> What you need to do is, when you want to abort and you might not be able to go to the clinic or the hospital, you must take a bottle of Old Brown [Sherry] and toilet paper or take newspaper and boil it and take that boiled newspaper and drink it and take a bucket that you normally use to pee in, undress and sit on it and all will come out. (Thulani, commercial farming area)

Many of the abortifacients are South African-made products – such as Oros or Oro Crush, a mostly artificial orange cordial, the household disinfectant Madubula, and Old Brown Sherry – or plants found in the field. Most of these products are relatively cheap and easy to come by, even in remote areas. Steel wool, also easy to obtain, is pushed up the vagina to facilitate the abortion. It seems to be believed that a household product can induce an abortion if it is toxic. As found in other research, these non-medical self-induction techniques seem to be widely known, with information on what to use and where to find plant abortifacients being passed on clandestinely from one person to another.[13]

KNOWLEDGE OF ABORTION PROCEDURES

Abortion procedures generally come in two forms: (1) medication (or medical) abortion, in which the pregnant woman ingests prescribed drugs (typically a combination of mifepristone and misoprostol); and (2) surgical abortion, a minor operation performed either through vacuum aspiration or dilation and curettage. Information about the procedures is meant to be provided in the initial consultation when a woman accesses abortion services. However, women in a study conducted in Cape Town by Marie Sullivan et al. indicated that they received little information regarding the type of abortion for which they were eligible.[14] Many women received incomplete information from referring clinics, and there were few personnel to answer questions.

Understandably, participants in our study spoke about abortion procedures in somewhat vague terms, as indicated below.

> The law I know is that before the doctor assists you with abortion, you have to fill in and sign a form acknowledging that you are going ahead with abortion and you have heard the risks involved. They, therefore, numb you with an injection so you don't feel pain. There is a machine that they switch on. It counts. As you are fast asleep, it cuts itself when it is time for you to wake up. If the machine

> doesn't go off at the right time, you die. These are some of the risks involved, and then if you are still sure you want to abort, they help you and receive their money. (Esihle, remote village)

> I will go to a doctor. We will sit down and talk; from there, he will go and examine if I may carry on with the procedure or not. After that, the doctor will tell me the details of how an abortion is done. Where you can have that blood clot moving around you. It then becomes necessary that we try and stop it from moving around. (Mthobeli, remote village)

Esihle refers here to informed consent, a procedure that is indeed necessary to obtain an abortion (and any other medical intervention). Most abortions, however, do not involve general anaesthesia and seldom lead to death if performed under safe conditions. Mthobeli also speaks vaguely about the procedure, moving on to other health concerns (blood clotting).

Some participants have been told frightening stories about late-term abortion procedures.

> Some say you must take the baby out and kill it by yourself. For example, if you mislead the abortion providers about how far along you are, maybe because you, too, were misled by an inaccurate pregnancy test. You then abort a baby that is alive, they then say kill him/her yourself, and then you kill him/her. (Esihle, remote village)

This participant understands the gestational limits for abortion on request. She indicates that people may be misled or lie about the gestation of a pregnancy. However, it is unlikely that abortion providers will inaccurately estimate a pregnancy's gestation. While the notion that providers will insist that women kill a live-born infant is incorrect, such renditions should perhaps be seen in the light of a general healthcare provider's negativity towards abortion. Research shows that many healthcare providers cite conscientious objection (or, as some would term it, refusal to care) concerning abortion.[15] Even those providing services may engage in talk that constructs abortion as 'at odds with moral values; unpleasant at best and harmful and dangerous at worst; and tolerable *only* as a last resort without more "preferable" pregnancy resolution alternatives, and when contraceptives have failed'.[16]

Participants also shared accounts of illegal and self-induced methods, sometimes going into graphic detail.

> If you drink a concoction to abort the pregnancy, you might bump into a lot of problems. If I take a mixture and don't get cleaned, I might get sick. Some pharmacies give abortion pills for R1 000 to sort out 'my problem'. I might lose strength on this bed without anyone to help after taking this pill because I do not want anyone to know what I have done. After the abortion has happened, I'll take the dead foetus, dig a grave and bury it. Or I can just throw it on the road. Then dogs can pick pieces of it apart and come to the people with it. (Fezeka, remote village)

> So, people don't have the necessary knowledge of what to do. Instead, they listen to others as they suggest pearls of pseudo-wisdom. They will say eat steel wool, Oro Crush, et cetera. And all these things will leave me damaged. I must just go to the hospital. They don't have such knowledge. I was also ignorant before my friend went for the abortion at the hospital. Another example is one of my other friends who once told me that she was pregnant and drank Flagyl. Do you know Flagyl [an antibiotic]? Flagyl is a pill that is used to clean the womb. She said she drank Flagyl, and I know how smelly Flagyl is. One tablet emits a very strong smell. How much more when you drink a packet? Some other people would say things that they think would work, never having seen it being done. One would just think that such-and-such a thing could damage the pregnancy. And it ends up being ineffective. It leaves you with some damage. (Thato, rural town)

These extracts illustrate participants' knowledge of the risks attached to unsafe abortion. Fezeka speaks to illness and loss of vitality. This, accompanied by the need for secrecy, may, according to Fezeka, descend into horror (dogs eating foetal remains and presenting these to other people). Thato talks about the physical damage that may result in hospitalisation. She argues that this happens because people lack an accurate understanding of self-inducing an abortion.

In these extracts, the participants are referring to self-managed abortions. As outlined by Joanna Erdman et al., there are three primary understandings of self-managed abortions: (1) an act of desperation, in which people are forced to self-induce because of restrictive legislation or dysfunctional health systems (the latter is the case in South Africa); (2) something that requires programmes and practices to reduce the risks and potential harm without prohibiting the activity itself; and (3) a purposeful act, rather than a desperate act or less desirable option, for which people must be treated with trust and respect.[17] The first perspective is reflected in the extracts cited above. Feminist organisations around the world have taken up the second perspective. They support pregnant women in self-managing their abortions, especially in places where abortion is restricted. They provide people with evidence-based information on the effective and safe use of abortion pills, which are accessed online or through local pharmacies. This approach became increasingly crucial during Covid-19 lockdowns.[18] To our knowledge, this kind of support is unavailable in the communities where we conducted our research. Given the concerns laid out in this book, such an approach may bear fruit. We discuss this further in the concluding chapter.

INFORMATION SOURCES ON ABORTION SERVICES

Research shows that people's sources of knowledge about abortion service provision vary according to the type of abortion sought. In a study by Caitlin Gerdts et al., most of the women participants who had accessed illegal abortions cited other community members and family members who had previously had an abortion as their source of information about informal sector abortion.[19] Signs and flyers offering *illegal* services (usually with the claim of being pain-free and safe) and posted in public areas frequented by many people (such as taxi ranks) also served as an important source of information. Print media, radio, television and internet searches are sources of information used to understand *legal* abortion services.

Women seeking an abortion may use the internet to search for nearby clinics or clinics in other towns. This can come with risks, however. For example, in a study by Jane Harries et al., some women indicated that, after searching online for clinics that provided abortion, they decided not to use the facilities because the 'clinics' were actually illegal providers. This was after 'making initial telephonic contact or, in two instances, after visiting the provider.'[20]

Our participants were asked where in the community they could find information on what to do when someone wants an abortion. Most mentioned that you can get information from people around you or from nurses at the clinic.

> We have information; we get it from each other, from people who have gone to certain abortion facilities. (Esihle, remote village)
>
> Living here, I think someone would have to ask around about the place in [distant city] that assists in having an abortion because, honestly, having an abortion the traditional way is not safe. (Khethiwe, remote village)
>
> I think it's something they hear. Maybe someone else had done it and survived. Or maybe someone else had used something, and they came out okay. I think they just hear it around. (Esona, rural town)

Local knowledge is spoken of here as a source of information. People who have had an abortion are considered reliable sources, especially if they 'survived'.

Clinics and hospitals, however, were seen as the most reliable sources of knowledge.

> She went to consult her mother's cousin, who was working at the hospital at the time, to arrange for her to get abortion. (Bamanye, rural town)
>
> Normally people would get such information from the health clinics or from a known midwife in the community who is against abortion. (Tabisa, rural town)
>
> Yes, because we tell each other lies. We tell you to drink such-and-such. We possess little knowledge, which tends to be dangerous. I think the clinic will set you on the right track. I never heard that the local clinic conducts abortions. What I know is the hospital in town. But I would suggest that one starts making enquiries at the local clinic. Maybe when you realise that you are pregnant, you can indicate to the nursing sister that you do not want the baby. What can I do to come out of this situation? (Thato, rural town)

Here participants suggest that the public health system is the best source of information. Local, informal knowledge is seen as dangerous. Thato refers to the referral system that operates in public health, with clinic nurses being able to refer to other facilities. However, the difficulty with this approach is that public health service providers have been known to discourage women from seeking abortions. Staff at referral centres may put obstacles in the way of women seeking services, invoking metaphors of killing and making religious references.[21] In addition, women living with HIV in a country with a high incidence and prevalence of HIV report being actively dissuaded from accessing abortions.[22]

Others mentioned receiving information about abortion providers from pamphlets or posters. Some of these, however, are the posters advertising illegal services that festoon public areas in most South African towns.

> She got these pamphlets that say here is a place you can do abortion here. (Amahle, rural town)
>
> It's the ones that are not legal. They are on every poster in town. If someone doesn't want to go to the public clinic, they will call that number that's on the poster and get the information. (Lithalethu, rural town)

One participant said she would opt to speak to the local NGO.

> Also, [the health programme manager at the NGO] with us here helps us a lot when we are pregnant. I think a person can talk to her if she no longer wants the pregnancy. (Amanda, rural town)

Electronic sources, while not prominent, were also mentioned.

> We have no such assistance here. We are informed only by the radio and television that one can terminate a pregnancy if they go to a place that offers that service. Without them, we would not know. (Lwandisa, commercial farming area)
>
> You do it as you have heard through hearsay; you ask from others as to how to do abortion, and now that there is Facebook, you ask there, and you get an answer. You choose from the options mentioned, you go to the clinic and buy those tablets, or you drink that coffee. (Buyiswa, commercial farming area)
>
> I hear on social networks, but the best people are the nurses in clinics. Social networks such as Google are the ways of white people, but the best information comes from nurses. (Sandisiwe, rural town)

The response from Sandisiwe speaks to the trust that some community members put in nurses. The 'ways of white people' are viewed either with suspicion or as something economically out of reach, given that, on average, white people continue to be wealthier than black people in South Africa. It is not clear which applies in the above quote.

CONCLUSION

The participants in these rural areas mostly had a basic knowledge of the legal status of abortion (with a few exceptions). They were also familiar with self-managed, illegal and unsafe abortions. Traditional healers were known as abortion providers but were not trusted in this capacity. Knowledge of the CTOP Act stipulations, facility locations and abortion procedures was sketchy. Some false and catastrophising narratives of abortion procedures were evident. Community members (mostly) and nurses were seen as reliable sources of information. Electronic sources were scarcely mentioned, while some mentioned posters advertising illegal abortions.

The partiality of our participants' knowledge is not surprising, given the government's lacklustre official information-sharing about legal abortion. This is due partially to a general opposition to abortion and partially to the vagaries of international donors. South Africa relies heavily on outside funds for HIV and other reproductive health prevention efforts. This makes the country susceptible to political interference in these areas. For example, former US president Donald Trump's reinstatement of the Global Gag Rule, which banned organisations receiving US government funding from offering or referring women for abortions, resulted in many adverse effects, including a lack of information sharing.[23]

While holding true across the country, these factors are exacerbated in rural areas, where access to electronic means of communication is limited. While there is an advantage in community members and nurses being known and possibly trusted, such reliance also poses a potential threat: community members may spread false information, and public health service providers may be anti-abortion.

While knowledge and information are necessary conditions for autonomous decision making, they are not sufficient. Where women know about abortion legislation facilities and procedures, other barriers, such as stigma, religious qualms and gendered power relations, may still constrain them from seeking an abortion. It is to these issues that we turn in the chapters to follow. But first, we look at the abortion decision-making process itself.

2

Aborting a Pregnancy: The Complexity of the Decision-Making Process

The CTOP Act is premised on a human rights framework, extending to every pregnant person 'the right to choose whether to have an early, safe and legal termination of pregnancy' in the first trimester.[1] Thus, in the first 12 weeks of gestation, the locus of decision making is firmly placed in the pregnant person's hands. The locus of decision making shifts to the health service provider from the second trimester, with medical doctors making a decision about termination based on the person's mental or physical health, risk of foetal abnormalities, instances of rape or incest, and the impact of birth on the social and economic status of the pregnant person.

The autonomy of decision making given to a pregnant person is thus circumscribed by the gestation date. Given the time-based nature of the CTOP Act and the shortage of services for second-trimester abortions, early pregnancy detection and accurate gestational dating are essential. We address this below.

Once pregnancy has been established, the abortion decision-making process is complex and embedded within overlapping power relations. As highlighted in the extract from one of our participant interviews, there are multiple reasons why a woman may terminate a pregnancy.

> I understand. And even the ones I used to blame in hospital I no longer blame now because it has come to me that they were aborting because the grant is small. They were aborting because they don't work. They were aborting because the boyfriend or husband says it's not his baby. They were aborting because it is rape. Because I had never given myself time to ask them, but I just told myself that they are cruel, but today I have reasons. I know why they performed an abortion. (Amanda, rural town)

The reasons why a woman might choose an abortion was a topic most participants engaged with robustly and one which often ended up in self-reflection, as seen in the extract above. In this chapter, we first discuss the most prominent interactions, reported as partner-related, that were said by participants to precipitate the decision to abort. We then discuss the multiple other reasons referred to by participants, such as poverty, family attitudes, multiple partners and casual sex.

The overtly stated reasons for abortion have been relatively widely studied; they include financial concerns, the need to complete schooling, inability to care for a(nother) child, lack of support and socially unacceptable pregnancy (for example, out of wedlock), among others. However, relatively little research has been conducted on the social dynamics involved in abortion decision making.[2] Family, selected friends, community members and partners play a significant role in women's decisions about the outcome of a pregnancy. This influence may be direct (e.g., through conversations about the situation) or indirect (e.g., through the women, especially young or unmarried women, being too scared to reveal the pregnancy or their intention to terminate it).[3] We concentrate in this chapter on interactions that circumscribe abortion decision making as related by our participants.

PARTNER-RELATED INTERACTIONS IN DECISION MAKING

The most prominent dynamics participants identified for women choosing an abortion were connected to the conception partner. This reflects findings by Marie Sullivan et al., who interviewed women who had undergone an abortion in the Western Cape. One woman 'didn't tell her partner about the abortion, fearing he would not be supportive'. Others cited relationship concerns, including lack of trust, as in the case of a cheating partner who did not want anything to do with the woman's pregnancy or an alcoholic partner who would not be a trusted father, as well as recent divorce or not being ready to raise a child with a new partner.[4]

Participants mentioned that unmarried women are vulnerable when an unplanned pregnancy occurs. They continually pointed out that men could simply deny the pregnancy, leave or insist on the abortion. Generally, men were described negatively, but even more so when it came to providing support during pregnancy, especially outside of marriage.

> I think that [choosing to abort] would be because of the hurt they would have experienced from their partner because the partner would deny impregnating her. (Anathi, remote village)
>
> [In the event of an unplanned pregnancy] the guy is going to deny that he impregnated me, and then we end up having an abortion. (Athule, rural town)
>
> My daughter is being beaten by her boyfriend. He says she must go do a DNA test. Our children are in relationships with very rude children … My child's boyfriend is denying the child. He is busy with other girls and abusing my child. (Bongezwa, commercial farming area)
>
> I never told my dad. I told my mother and said I'm aborting this first pregnancy because the reason is that the father of this child is denying that he impregnated me. My mother said, 'If you say so, then that is fine because I'm also not working.' As you can see,

> I'm also sick. And my dad is also not working, and so my dad said, 'Okay, abort, my child, there's no problem.' (Thulani, commercial farming area)

Bongezwa and Thulani draw on both personal experience and knowledge of community dynamics to outline how paternity denial plays into the decision to terminate a pregnancy. This denial leads to 'hurt', abuse, and difficulties around financial support. The question of paternity denial has been raised in other studies. For example, in the context of studying alcohol use during pregnancy in the Eastern Cape, participants described consuming alcohol to relieve stress resulting from partners denying paternity.[5]

Participants indicated that having multiple partnerships makes women especially vulnerable since sexual partners are even more likely to deny paternity; women also fear that knowledge of the infidelity might end their main relationship.

> In a situation like this one [multiple partners], that is where abortion is necessary. For example, I personally didn't get pregnant by my main boyfriend. I got pregnant by someone else. I really wanted to abort the child then but didn't know what to do. (Khethiwe, remote village)
>
> It becomes worse when I get pregnant under such circumstances, having other boyfriends. And my boyfriend is having other girlfriends. That could cause me to take a decision on my own to do it [an abortion]. Because I would not be certain as to who the father of the child is, due to that I have other boyfriends on the side. (Thato, rural town)
>
> The reason … I made a decision to abort the first child, my husband's family said the child isn't my husband's and therefore I decided to abort rather than to keep a child that I don't even know who the father was, you understand? (Thulani, commercial farming area)

These participants suggest the following outcomes in the case of pregnancy in the context of multiple partnerships, all of which may lead to a decision to terminate the pregnancy: fear of not knowing who the conception partner is, judgement from the community, and pressure from the main partner's family or from one of the partners. Proof of paternity was seen as paramount.

Denial of paternity can be viewed as a form of reproductive coercion. Reproductive coercion has been defined as 'behaviour aimed at establishing and maintaining power and control over a person, by interfering with their reproductive autonomy, denying them control, decision-making and access to options regarding reproductive health choices'.[6] According to participants, such coercion may also take the form of partners using relationship continuation and finances as incentives to have an abortion.

> Normally, it does happen sometimes that when you are pregnant the father of the baby is adamant that he does not want the baby. (Ziyanda, commercial farming area)
>
> Are you going to keep the baby after having been told that he does not want one? He will say here's the money, go and abort ... The male partner takes the decision and you play along because you are pleasing him. I am protecting the relationship. Because my partner says, here's the money, go and abort because I am too busy for a child. Then you realise that this person does not want the child. It is your partner. You are still hoping to continue with the relationship. He gives you the money, he does not just say I do not want the baby and abandons you. He says he does not want the child and he puts his purse on the table. It is what makes one to go and terminate the pregnancy. (Thato, rural town)

Thato paints a detailed picture of a male partner's insistence on an abortion, neatly laying out the gender dynamics around access to financial resources. Given the premium on financial resources in these poor areas, access to 'his purse' is seen as a sign of commitment. This, in contrast to paternity denial, gives hope for the relationship, which, as indicated by Thato, a pregnant woman has to weigh up against any desire she may have to take the pregnancy to term.

Women were also said to consider an abortion because they feared their partner would leave them. Abandonment was seen as most likely in the event of an unplanned pregnancy.

> When you encounter an unplanned pregnancy, the men leave you. Then you become stressed and lose the baby. Others choose abortion because they think their men will leave them, and they are not willing to have a fatherless child. (Esihle, remote village)
>
> It is circumstances of having no one to lean on, because you now become the sole parent of this child as the father runs away. Have you ever raised a child alone? It is horrible. (Funeka, remote village)
>
> Sometimes it's no different because sometimes even though you're married to a person, when you fall pregnant the partner leaves you or you break up and they never care about you whereas in the beginning they loved you. (Yamkela, rural town)
>
> In some situations, the father runs away, so you must find a job to support your child. (Mpendulo, rural town)

The stresses of partner abandonment are made clear here – miscarriage and single parenting, which requires both caring for the child and finding employment. Actual or potential threats of abandonment featured prominently in another study on abortion decision making in South Africa and Zimbabwe.[7]

In addition to physical abandonment, participants spoke about men being unable or unwilling to support the pregnancy and the child financially.

> Most times they do abortion the female does the abortion because the male says that he doesn't have money to raise the child since his parents are still paying for his education. (Aphiwe, remote village)

She told me that she can't stay with the child's father when he isn't doing anything for her. He can't even buy her toiletries or shoes, or clothes. That's why she wants to abort. (Thulani, commercial farming area)

Well, when they [the fathers] do not want the child, their friends can also influence them to abort because it can never, you know … He would not look after you, and they then end up terminating. (Ikhona, commercial farming area)

Maybe when her family does not accept [the pregnancy], you find that she is stressed now because she doesn't have support from family. Even the partner does not provide support, so you find that now in all this you feel alone and want now ways to relieve yourself so that you can move on with your life. (Amahle, rural town)

In these extracts, lack of financial support from the male partner is constructed as a major factor in the decision to terminate a pregnancy. Ikhona speaks to the anticipation among women's peers that men will not support them during pregnancy or childbearing, either financially or through practical assistance. This scenario is portrayed to women by their peers even before it happens, according to Ikhona, which suggests it is widely recognised.

Participants sometimes spoke of a cultural phenomenon known as *ukwaliswa* or *ukubukuzana* (often directly translated as 'the foetus does not want the father'). Esona Bottoman describes this phenomenon in her research on the pregnancy-support narratives of women living in a rural area of the Eastern Cape.[8] Men leave temporarily during pregnancy because of the woman's hormonal or mood changes. During this time, men may engage in other sexual activities, which are justified by normalising 'men's uncontrollable sexual desires'.[9] Men may return once the baby is born.

Some [couples] stay together until the baby is born. Some can even break up and be together again when the baby is born. Or they may not even want to sleep in the same room. You may not even want him next to you because he smells bad [body sweat] as if he didn't bath. (Sinoxolo, commercial farming area)

The woman develops things [when she is pregnant]. She starts having strange feelings on her tummy and feels nauseous and vomits. Her complexion changes. She gets cheeky. Sometimes she fights with her boyfriend. Something like that … Usually at that time, they are not on good terms. Only when she comes back with the baby are they on good terms again. The baby's mom calls the baby's father to tell him she has a baby, and they are back on good terms. (Yanela, commercial farming area)

This kind of abandonment is viewed as temporary and well understood by all parties. The return of the partner after the birth means that abortion is not necessary.

Participant discussion of paternity denial, partner abandonment or partner coercion to terminate a pregnancy painted pictures of hostile gender relations, with men being positioned as uncaring and irresponsible. Not all discussions depicted partners in negative ways, however. Participants also indicated that women might seek to terminate their pregnancy if the relationship with the conception partner was casual or not strong.

The thing is these children when they are disappointed by the father of the baby … the child would rather go to all of these hospitals. (Khunjulwa, remote village)

Maybe one of them wants the option of an abortion because they were not dating. Maybe a mistake had happened, and they ended up sleeping together, so the woman might want to opt for an abortion since she was not in love with the person who had made her pregnant. (Azole, rural town)

You see, according to me, I had these thoughts that 'Okay, this has happened, and I am not ready, and I don't like the father of this child'. The only thing that came to my mind was abortion. (Bongiwe, rural town)

Here unsuitable relationships ('I don't like the father') or casual relationships ('not dating') are seen as valid reasons for terminating a pregnancy. The relationship dynamics in these instances are not about coercion or lack of choice for financial reasons; instead, the woman makes a choice to have an abortion based on the status and quality of the relationship.

FAMILY-RELATED DYNAMICS

Families, especially parents, can be important support structures for people living in rural areas. However, according to participants, families may be hostile regarding unplanned pregnancies, and women may choose to have abortions out of fear of their response.

> Another one [reason for choosing abortion] would be because they fear their parents. (Bongani, remote village)
> Some abort because, at home, their father beats them every time they leave the house and threatens them with 'the day you get pregnant, you will know me'. So, a girl will see no other solution but to abort. (Fezeka, remote village)
> The woman was afraid of her family and of her partner as the partner was a bit older than herself. (Tabisa, rural town)
> I was scared of my mother because she is a quiet person, and I saw that she does not like this. I heard that she mentioned to my family that she hates what I did. (Athule, rural town)

Here participants speak about families' disapproval of and threats concerning unplanned pregnancies. Phrases such as 'you will know me' threaten physical violence, which the pregnant woman would want to avoid. Such fears of family reactions to unplanned pregnancies, mainly in the case of young women, have been documented in South African literature. For example, Sisa Ngabaza outlines how teenage pregnancies are 'framed within relationships of control, regulation and power, especially in relation to parental authority'.[10]

Participants provided various reasons for family disapproval of youthful pregnancy, including the fear that shame will accrue to the family, religious reasons and financial concerns.

> It is bad, but some parents do such things. They would see that the child is still young and will bring the reputation of the family into disrepute, and they will be the laughing stock of the village. (Lithalethu, rural town)
>
> She was a child still at school and was embarrassed to be seen at school pregnant, so her mom gave her the money to go to those places [abortion providers], and she came back to school. (Yanga, commercial farming area)
>
> For some women, it could be that their families are religious. In such a case as when a young woman falls pregnant, she may choose a place where her parents will not find out about the abortion and will also have no influence on the outcome of the pregnancy. (Simbongile, rural town)
>
> Family members and the community perceive unwanted pregnancy as wrong. If a student gets pregnant, it's problematic that she fell pregnant, because who is going to look after the child, who is going to feed the child because the social grant is not enough. On the other side, the father is probably a student/learner too. (Bamanye, rural town)

These participants speak to the question of shame and people's actions to avoid shame. Shame accrues around a sense of being judged by others or the self as being unworthy or wrong, acting in unacceptable ways or being complicit in the suffering of others.[11] In the first and second extracts above, shame is depicted as accruing to the family and the young woman because of the pregnancy. As pointed out by Michalinos Zembylas, shame may result in practices of concealment.[12] In these instances, abortion is the means of concealing a shameful pregnancy. The third extract depicts women concealing an abortion due to the family's religious sensibilities. In the fourth extract, the moral status of the pregnancy is called into question (it is 'wrong'), but for different reasons – financial and caregiving stresses.

The references in these extracts to the difficulties concerning young pregnant women who are still in school resonate with the scholarly critique that schools fail to provide sufficient support for pregnant and childbearing learners. Even though it is illegal to expel learners from schools based on their pregnancy status, many pregnant learners experience exclusionary practices, including stigmatising talk by teachers and principals, teasing by learners and lack of support for their learning requirements. These practices are premised on the basis that 'the school is constructed as a space where pregnancy and parenting are unintelligible'.[13]

While for the most part family influence was portrayed as above – that is, women terminating the pregnancy to avoid strong family disapproval – some participants spoke about families actively coercing women into abortion.

> It depends. Sometimes, people terminate pregnancy because the family took that decision on their behalf. Some families ask their children to do an abortion because they feel humiliated that their child fell pregnant at a very young age. It might happen that they never wanted to have an abortion in the first place. People who have aborted can't just be ignored; they should be offered support because they might be dying inside. However, families don't consider that. They just decide that it's going to be a secret between the family while the child might be hurting and is in need of support. (Athenkosi, commercial farming area)

Shame plays a particular part in this narrative of abortion coercion. The family feels 'humiliated' and decides on a course of action to reduce this humiliation. Instead of supporting the young person in making their own decision, they protect the family's reputation by concealing the pregnancy and taking a 'decision on their behalf' to have an abortion. This pattern of families coercing women to perform an abortion has been reported in research in the USA, where Lauren Ralph et al. found that, compared with adults, minors were more likely to report external pressure, especially from mothers, to seek an abortion.[14]

POVERTY AND THE DECISION TO ABORT

According to participants, a major factor in the decision to abort is the woman's fear that she cannot afford to care for a child or another child.

> Not having much. The one thing that scares a person from having a baby is not having anything. A child is an expense because they have to be supported even when they are still in the tummy. (Kuhle, remote village)
>
> Other situations could be that one wants the baby, but there's no money to support it. Yes, there are grants but, in some families, they are struggling even with the help of grants. So maybe someone thinks of those matters. (Lithalethu, rural town)
>
> This is because some youth abort because they are concerned about their home's poverty and wonder what the child will eat if they keep it. Then friends will advise abortion to get out of the difficult situation. (Akhona, remote village)
>
> Some ill-treat you because they wonder why you would get pregnant knowing that your family is poor. And they will say things to you, and you will realise that this is hurting you. Then some decide to abort the baby. (Sinoxolo, commercial farming area)

These participants' responses illustrate the complexities surrounding poverty in pregnancy. High levels of unemployment make abortion a distinct possibility for women living in rural areas. Family financial resources tend to be minimal, and the child support grant (R720 per child per month at the time of writing) does little to alleviate the hardships. The expenses incurred during pregnancy and in looking after a child (particularly if there are other children) are considered prohibitive in such contexts. Akhona and Sinoxolo refer to the social recognition of these factors. Akhona mentions support from friends, while Sinoxolo discusses adverse reactions from community members to pregnancy in the context of poverty.

The importance of economic concerns in terminating a pregnancy is recognised in the CTOP Act. One of the conditions under which second-trimester abortion may be performed is if 'the continued pregnancy would significantly affect the social or economic circumstances of the woman'.[15] The fact that continued pregnancy may, in many instances, harm the economic circumstances of women has been well established in the Turnaway Study conducted in the USA.[16] The Turnaway Study was a five-year longitudinal observational study that followed two groups of women: (1) women who were denied abortion because they were beyond the gestational age limit in their legislative environment, and (2) women who received an abortion just before the gestational age limit. Children born to the former group of women were compared to subsequent children born to the latter group of women. The children of the former group lived in households with lower incomes than the children of the latter group and were more likely to live in households without enough money to pay for basic living expenses. In other words, when women are denied a wanted abortion, the children they give birth to fare poorly economically.

POOR ANTENATAL AND PERINATAL CARE, AND THE DECISION TO ABORT

Antenatal care clinics tend to be overcrowded and their services overstretched in South Africa, despite the Department of Health's significant efforts to improve prenatal care to reduce maternal mortality and morbidity.[17] In rural areas, this is exacerbated by the distance women must travel to reach public health clinics. Participants indicated that some women might choose abortion over a pregnancy because pregnancy is stressful and expensive.

> So, a person can have an abortion because the whole pregnancy will be a difficult journey because of the lack of accessibility to healthcare facilities that are close by. (Gcobisa, remote village)
>
> They must be constantly monitored and checked via the tv [scans] to see if the baby that is carried is okay. That is the first step. In our village, we do not have those kinds of safety measures so that a child can be seen in the early stages of pregnancy [to judge] if they are okay. We need those kinds of things here. (Kuhle, remote village)
>
> The clinic is far away from here. We have to take transport every time. When you do not have money, it becomes a struggle, and the clinic beyond [in the next village] is far from us. When we are pregnant, it's hard to walk … so we are then forced to take a car to go to [another village]. (Mafungwashe, remote village)

These participants, all from the most remote site, bemoan the lack of antenatal care facilities close to their village. They are aware of the need for antenatal care, but distance creates a barrier to obtaining it. Kuhle comments on how inaccessibility affects the health management of the pregnancy. Mafungwashe refers to the cost implications (having to pay for transport as walking is too difficult). Indeed, research shows that women in rural areas report significantly more barriers to antenatal care than women in urban areas.[18] This results in more rural- than urban-based women presenting late for antenatal care.

The distance to hospitals and maltreatment by service providers during prenatal care were also mentioned.

> I would like to have children, but because I was mistreated [at the hospital], I took a decision that, no, I will never have children again

because I think that maybe this time, if I have a child again, the child would live, and I would die. So, I took a decision that let me stay with the child I already have. (Boipelo, commercial farming area)

I do not know. They also discourage me at the hospitals. A person will go to the hospital to give birth, and they will just get shouted at at that hospital. (Bongani, remote village)

Even when you get to town, you catch a taxi for R10 from town to [another larger town]. There is the hospital. Then that is where they will check on the scan if the baby is positioned right and what sex they are. They see everything. Then during labour, that is the hardest time, that time you can call the ambulance. Let's say you felt the baby coming at 3 a.m. You can call the ambulance until 7 a.m. That is when it is hardest. Some people hire a car to take them to [large town] because they do not do childbirth at the clinic. It is done at the hospital in [large town]. Most of the time, the locals hire cars to help … but they are also not always available when you call. It's not there because it may be taking someone else to the hospital, you see? You are having contractions. This is really the hardest time. (Siphamandla, rural town)

Boipelo outlines how the maltreatment she received from healthcare providers during birth (which she later described in depth in the interview) made her determined never to have another child. Bongani refers to being shouted at during birth. This kind of treatment has been called obstetric violence and is well documented in South Africa.[19] Siphamandla refers an additional stress during birth – the possibility of an ambulance or private transport not being available to take women to the hospital when labour starts. While the state ambulance would not incur costs for the woman's family, hiring private transport would.

These findings are important in relation to abortion decision making. They suggest that it is not only partner-, family- or poverty-related dynamics which feed into abortion decision making but also experiences and expectations of pregnancy and birth care. Our participants suggest that in the context of significant distance and cost in accessing pregnancy and birth care, which may be disrespectful and at times violent, abortion may be considered a better option.

CONCLUSION

A comparative study of South African and Zimbabwean women's narratives of the decision-making process regarding abortion found that women felt obligated to justify their abortion decision in the interactive interview space.[20] This indicates that the decision was not considered ordinary or part of standard reproductive healthcare decision making. The justificatory labour engaged in by the participants in the 2017 study by Chiweshe et al. centred on relationships (including lack of marriage, the imperative of good mothering, and unstable partner relationships) rather than reproductive health rights. This is in line with international literature, where researchers in the USA,[21] the UK[22] and Kenya[23] found that women's reasons for abortion centre on a concern for or consideration of others and that prevailing understandings of responsibility played an important role in the decision-making process.

In this chapter, we outlined how our participants depicted abortion decision making as heavily steeped in partner and family relationships. Fears of paternity denial, partner abandonment, lack of partner support, the discovery of multiple relationships, family disapproval and shame accruing to the family were all represented as important factors in the decision-making process. Examples of reproductive coercion, in which partners or family members strongly urge the pregnant person to undergo an abortion, were also discussed.

Structural issues relating to poverty and lack of antenatal and perinatal care access also featured in the participants' talk. Our research was carried out in resource-poor contexts, and it is unsurprising that financial resources featured significantly in decision-making discussions. The general lack of employment and state-provided resources (such as accessible antenatal and perinatal care) looms large in these people's lives. An important finding is that it is not only the distance to and the cost of accessing antenatal and perinatal care that featured in participants' talk. Obstetric violence, defined as 'abusive practices in obstetric care settings',[24] was also considered a possible factor in abortion decision making.

In the following chapter, we turn to community reactions and attitudes towards unintended pregnancies and abortion. Together with the inter-personal relationships and structural issues outlined in this chapter, socially embedded narratives about both pregnancy and abortion form the backdrop against which decisions regarding the outcome of pregnancy are made.

3

Sin, Injury and Discord: Community Attitudes and Understandings of Abortion

Research in South Africa indicates that overall public support for abortion is low, with few people approving abortion on request or for social and economic reasons.[1] There is, however, some support for abortion in cases of rape, incest or danger to the pregnant person's health.[2] Support (or lack thereof) is not even across all population groups. For example, a survey among university students found that, compared to male students, female students had more positive attitudes towards women's autonomy in abortion decision making and towards making abortion accessible.[3] Indeed, the gendered aspect of public understanding of abortion has been highlighted in several studies.[4] In addition, religion plays a major role in abortion attitudes.[5]

In our study, several questions in the participant interviews probed community perceptions on topics related to abortion. The following themes emerged in relation to these questions: abortion is 'not right';

abortion is murder; an abortion means killing a child with a potentially bright future; and abortion has physical and mental health consequences, including infertility. Many participants reported that community members held different beliefs on abortion, and some indicated that there were situations in which abortion should be legal. There were also discussions on how communities should consider being less judgemental and aim to understand women's situations.

ANTI-ABORTION SENTIMENT: MORAL ARGUMENTS

Participants often spoke of either themselves or community members seeing abortion as not being 'right'.

> When I see people who get pregnant for a long period of time with a living human being in them, then at the end you find out that they did an abortion – that is not right. (Bathandwa, remote village)
>
> There is no such thing as an argument about whether or not your abortion is legal. It is just thought that they shouldn't abort. It is not about the legalities. It is about their opinion that you shouldn't abort. (Andisiwe, rural town)

These participants argue that abortion, even if legal, should not take place. Their statements were not nuanced or couched in softening language. Instead, the 'fact' was simply stated.

For the most part, the unacceptability of abortion rested on religious beliefs, in which abortion is equated with murder.

> People have different faiths and beliefs. We believe aborting a child is killing an innocent soul. (Bamanye, rural town)
>
> Whether you are married or not, keep the baby. Don't terminate the pregnancy; that is a sin. (Bongezwa, commercial farming area)
>
> Because she killed a person, so when she can kill a person that is not right, she is a bad person. (Bathandwa, remote village)

> Yes, for example in the church they emphasise a lot about abortion. My pastor even tells you that you are leaving a trail of dead bodies of children that you have aborted. (Siphamandla, rural town)

> People who have abortions should just be arrested and locked away. They are doing a lot of damage to themselves. (Bongani, remote village)

> When you have an abortion, you have committed a huge crime of killing a child. You should not be compensated. If anything, you must head to jail. (Khunjulwa, remote village)

Bongezwa alludes to the pressure that a pregnancy outside of wedlock could place on a woman to terminate the pregnancy. But she indicates that yielding to this pressure is unacceptable because to undergo an abortion is a sin. The reason it is a sin is expanded upon by Bamanye, Bathandwa, Siphamandla and Khunjulwa: abortion is an act of killing. For some, such as Bongani and Khunjulwa, having an abortion justifies sending the woman to jail.

The status of the foetus, or when life begins, has been a key element in the politics of abortion worldwide. Much of the vociferous debate concerning abortion has centred on the right of the foetus to life versus the right of the pregnant person to bodily integrity. This bifurcation has led to the labelling of various groups as 'pro-life' and 'pro-choice'. Even though these bifurcated positions do not do justice to the complexities of the debate, they persist. Moreover, neither of these positions is without contradictions. For example, as pointed out by Kristin Luker, self-labelled pro-life antagonists are seldom completely rigid about saving foetal life. Often, for example, they will concede that abortion may be morally acceptable in cases of rape or incest.[6]

For the most part, pro-choice activists have concentrated on the rights of pregnant people to make decisions about the outcome of a pregnancy. However, as Anuradha Kumar points out:

> Now that anti-choice groups have been allowed to frame the rhet-oric about women who have abortions and abortion providers,

the challenge for reproductive rights advocates is to acknowledge that abortion leads to a form of death or the loss of a potential life while at the same time asserting women's moral agency to cause that death or loss.[7]

The key phrase here is 'a form of death'. While the foetus remains non-viable, it is the product of conception – not a separate human life – that undergoes death within the pregnant person's body.

Viability, or the gestational age at which a foetus can survive outside the uterus, is sometimes seen as the moral cut-off point for a termination of pregnancy (TOP). This is often cited as being at 24 weeks of gestation. However, actual viability very much depends on the medical resources and technologies available to the pregnant person. While legislation in some countries provides gestational date cut-off points for legal abortions, other countries use 'viability' as a yardstick. For example, the Irish government allows abortions when there is a risk to the life or health of the pregnant woman *and* the foetus has not reached viability. Viability is defined in this legislation as 'the point in a pregnancy at which, in the reasonable opinion of a medical practitioner, the foetus is capable of survival outside the uterus without extraordinary life-sustaining measures'.[8]

Potential human life, as referred to by Kumar[9] above, was taken up by participants. In opposing abortion, participants frequently spoke about children with a potentially bright future.

> They [the community] feel bad about it. It worries them. Because that child that they have aborted could have been their only child, or they were going to become a teacher, or they were going to become a person who helps a lot of people. (Bongani, remote village)
>
> The issue is that abortions are not good. Maybe you are aborting a future lawyer or nurse or whatever and you don't know what the future had in store for that child. (Fezeka, remote village)

> And if you abort you will never know if that child was going to be the right one out of the ones you did not abort. (Bamanye, rural town)

These comments speak to the value attached to children and their potential. Research in South Africa shows that families ascribe social, emotional and practical value to children – often in equal measure.[10] Social value refers to children's active participation in community interactions and cultural practices; emotional value means the child is cherished as a unique individual; and practical value refers to children's current contribution to family labour and future income generation. The participants above refer to all three forms of value ('helps a lot of people' = social value; 'be the right one' = emotional value; 'a future lawyer or nurse' = practical value). According to these participants, these potentialities or values of children mean that abortion is simply wrong.

ANTI-ABORTION SENTIMENTS: DAMAGE ARGUMENTS

Abortion was opposed not only on moral grounds but also because of the damage it causes to self or others. Damage was spoken about in general terms but also in relation to infertility and psychological and social fallout.

> The people who get abortions – in my opinion getting an abortion should not be important [should not be done] because having an abortion when you are young is also going to affect you mentally. Your body is going to tell that something is missing … Having an abortion is wrong, because we can physically tell that something is wrong or missing from looking at you. Even if you went behind everyone's back and got an abortion, we can tell, and we can see what you have done. Nothing good comes from having an abortion. (Khunjulwa, remote village)
>
> Maybe they [the women] could die, or they could become very ill when they have an abortion, you see? Maybe you would never be all right like you were before you aborted … What happens is

that you suddenly see a person just drained of life, you see them looking weak. Maybe their whole body was beautiful, it was all right, and then you see that they are no longer the picture of health anymore. (Bongani, remote village)

In these extracts, undefined 'damage' includes possible mental health consequences, death, illness, weakness and ill health. According to Bongani and Khunjulwa, these ill effects cannot be hidden. Community members can perceive that a woman who has aborted is 'no longer the picture of health', and they will be able to see 'what you have done'.

Researchers have commented on the emphasis on damage in opposing abortion. Alexa Trumpy, for example, refers to a frame shift in which the anti-abortion movement began replacing foetal-centric rhetoric with talk claiming that abortion harms women.[11] Anti-abortion advocates who rely solely on the right of a foetus to life can be accused of lacking empathy with or understanding of pregnant people's lives and circumstances. Incorporating arguments about the (alleged) physical and psychological harm that women will face when having an abortion enables anti-abortionists to position themselves as protecting women and, hence, their stance as woman-centred.

The harm most emphasised by our participants was that of of infertility, including in cases of rape (which was seen in many instances as an acceptable reason to obtain an abortion). The decision not to terminate the pregnancy was seen as premised on the possibility of not being able to conceive in future.

Maybe I could be aborting my last child and I won't be able to conceive in the future when I want a child. My only chance at being a parent I lost when I threw the baby away. (Fezeka, remote village)

Some would keep the baby because of the fear of infertility in the future and end up adopting and doing other things. (Bamanye, rural town)

So, a woman may have an abortion because she was raped and did not want a child, you understand? But mostly, you must understand what she wants because, as I said, some complications may arise during an abortion. Not only that, but she may want to abort a child only to find out later that it was her one and only child and she would never have another one. (Simbongile, rural town)

These participants' responses should be contextualised within South Africa's deeply pronatalist culture, in which women are strongly encouraged to have children. Those who do not have children often face stigma and discrimination.[12] Phrases like 'I threw the baby away' and 'she would never have another' point to the premium placed on children.

Infertility was described as a result of damage to the uterus, as well as God's retribution.

When you want a child, your womb will have been used to you aborting and you will miscarry. (Esona, rural town)

Even though you have gone to a doctor and performed a legitimate procedure of termination, there are still chances of you not being able to have another child again after you have terminated a baby before. Then, sometime after you have done termination, when you are wanting to have a baby again and you try to conceive, after three months you will have a miscarriage because of the damage to your uterus caused by the termination. (Bulelani, rural town)

You should not get an abortion. It [the pregnancy] is a gift from God. Where will you get another child? Because we grew up being told if you get an abortion, you will not be able to have children again. And you will go to hell all because of your own wrongdoings. (Thato, remote village)

When you are pregnant, the body is aware there is something else within the body and prepares itself. When you are terminating a pregnancy, there might be other things that leave [your body] with the termination. Perhaps in due time you will not be all right, it isn't done right, or your health is affected. Maybe your chance is gone, and Father God says, 'I had given you your chance and I won't give you another'. (Sandisiwe, rural town)

Here participants refer to uteri that have suffered 'damage' or are 'used to' abortion, which results in the miscarriage of future pregnancies. In addition, God may punish a woman for undergoing an abortion by preventing the birth of future children.

In the contexts within which our research was conducted, these damage-related sentiments may be compounded by the outcomes associated with unsafe abortion practices, with which participants may be acquainted. There certainly are many physical harms to unsafe abortion (and possibly psychological harms, although this is not well studied). Indeed, according to the World Health Organization (WHO), unsafe abortion is 'a leading – but preventable – cause of maternal deaths and morbidities'.[13] In contrast, legal, safe abortions, both pharmaceutical and surgical, are among the safest medical procedures available. Abortion conducted under safe circumstances is, as outlined in a review by Sam Rowlands, 'clearly safer than childbirth'.[14] His survey shows no evidence of an association between abortion and breast cancer or infertility. Moreover, women who have abortions are not at increased risk of mental health problems over and above those faced by women who deliver an unwanted pregnancy.[15] Nevertheless, the notion that one could die or become ill due to abortion (even if performed legally, as stated by Bulelani above) has taken on a life of its own and fuels abortion stigma (see the discussion in chapter 4).

ABORTION: A DISPUTED ISSUE

Despite participants' general negativity towards abortion, they indicated that abortion was a disputed subject in the community. The answer to whether all community members held the same beliefs regarding abortion was always no. Different people had different opinions.

Others encourage you to get an abortion, others discourage that because they don't like it when you terminate a soul. (Esihle, remote village)

They have different views because one says you are playing with death when you terminate while others say it's not a problem. (Kuhle, remote village)

They know that a person has the right to do an abortion when she wants to go through the right channels, and then other people – you can see that they have that thing that you can't do an abortion because the child is a blessing from God. (Amahle, rural town)

As with any social issue, it is expected and acknowledged by these participants that there will be varying views on the matter.

Some dispute seems to revolve around the circumstances in which abortion is acceptable. Provisional acceptance of abortion (for instance, when performed on particular grounds) was mentioned several times by participants.

[Abortion is acceptable in] circumstances where someone is poor, and they do not know what they will do with the baby. (Siphamandla, rural town)

What can I say? I think they [unmarried pregnant women] are treated differently. When you're married, you must have a child, but when you're not married, having a child is not right. This is where I think the abortion is needed. (Khethiwe, remote village)

As I said, what if this is your last chance at having a child? It doesn't matter the reason, but what matters [is that] you are aborting a child. We do know, though, that people do things for different reasons. Some abort because at home their father beats them. (Fezeka, remote village)

Yes. We spoke about rape. So, it could be legal in that case. I would like it to be legal in that case, but it still requires the pregnant woman to decide whether she wants to have an abortion or not. (Simbongile, rural town)

Here abortion is seen as acceptable only under certain circumstances, including being poor, unwed, or the victim of rape or of violence in the home. Simbongile talks about rape being a legitimate reason for abortion but intimates that it is not a simple decision. Indeed, rape featured strongly in the discussions, with some complex reasoning surfacing. This is discussed further below.

Some of the participants espoused tolerance of abortion.

A person terminates a pregnancy because of their situation which they understand. I don't think it's legal; it's just situations are different. (Kuhle, remote village)

I think the community needs to stop being judgemental, as we all are not perfect in life. We make mistakes and learn from them. Everyone has his/her own mistakes, so we should not judge. (Bamanye, rural town)

There are some who do understand that it might have been certain circumstances that influenced someone to go and get an abortion. (Ntobeko, rural town)

Yes, the community would look at her in a bad way, but it is none of their business, because a decision is made by the person and it's her liking. (Amanda, rural town)

Arguments for abortion tolerance appearing in these extracts include the ideal of being non-judgemental; an understanding of the pregnant person's situation; being forgiving of mistakes; and the idea that it is the woman's decision. Statements referring to the woman's choice, such as that made by Amanda, were few and far between. Although the language of rights is not used here, the implication is that women should be allowed to make their own decisions about their bodies. The lack of traction of a rights-based discourse in the talk of women presenting for abortion in the Eastern Cape is commented on by Malvern Chiweshe et al. In their analysis, women sought to justify their abortions but never with the language of rights.[16]

ATTITUDES TOWARDS RAPE VICTIMS WHO ABORT

As indicated above, rape was seen by participants as a legitimate reason for choosing an abortion. Most participants indicated that communities were in favour of abortion in the case of rape. There were, however, nuances in the responses, as indicated below.

A few participants used the language of 'choice' to indicate that it would be the rape victim's decision whether or not to abort.

> I would say that it depends on her. If she doesn't want to keep the baby, maybe because it will remind her of what happened, she can take that decision. (Lithalethu, rural town)
>
> Yes, or they [her family] will ask her what she wants to do, whether she wants an abortion or not. (Anelisa, commercial farming area)
>
> The decision lies with the victim whether or not she keeps the child. She will decide. (Tsepiso, commercial farming area)
>
> They can't force her to keep the baby or force her to abort when she feels different about it. It's all dependent on the person carrying the baby. (Linda, commercial farming area)

This kind of exceptionalism around rape as a valid reason for abortion is not uncommon. Many countries with restrictive legislation do allow abortion in cases of rape. Some, however, require a police report, which is a barrier to rape victims accessing abortion. It is well known that only a fraction of rapes get reported. For example, in South Africa, it is estimated that about 1 in 9 women who experience rape report the crime to the police. (Of those reporting, suspects are arrested in about half the cases; and of those arrested, under half are charged. Trials commence in fewer than 1 in 6 cases, and the conviction rate is about 1 in 20 cases.)[17]

The stigma that usually attaches itself to abortion (discussed in detail in the following chapter) was seen by participants as being mitigated in the case of rape.

> Then if the pregnancy is the result of rape and you abort it, it's seen as the right and acceptable thing to do by the community members. (Khethiwe, remote village)
>
> I don't think that they will judge her much, considering that the pregnancy is due to rape. (Azole, rural town)
>
> They [the community] understand because [the woman was] raped and did not ask for a child but got raped. (Yanga, commercial farming area)
>
> It will be difficult to judge that in a bad light. Let's say 90% of the community will support that action. Because this person was raped, they were not lovers. He just wants to spoil the child's future … But the community will not put blame on her. The only problematic section of the community could be the elders. Elderly people are used to sugar-coating terrible deeds. (Thato, rural town)

Here the participants indicate general community support for abortion due to rape. Thato, however, provides a caveat that 10% of the community may not 'support that action', particularly the elders. Instead, she suggests, they will cover things up.

Participants indicated that not only would stigma not accrue to women who terminate a pregnancy in the case of rape, but active support and compassion may be provided.

> Perhaps let's say she has found herself pregnant. She then decides to terminate the pregnancy as she doesn't want the baby to serve as a reminder of what has happened to her. Or [if] she decided to

keep the baby, what we need to do as a family is to support her. (Lithalethu, rural town)

The people in the community are normally compassionate towards both the child and mother. (Tabisa, rural town)

They [community members] don't take it badly because they know what happened. You got raped, so they know you didn't get raped because you wanted to. So they'll support you. (Mpendulo, rural town)

Here participants talk about support and compassion for the woman who does not want to be reminded of the rape (through bearing a child) and the understanding that she is in no way responsible for the rape.

Several justifications were provided for the necessity of abortion in the case of rape. These frequently had to do with the poor outcomes expected of children conceived by rape, such as they cannot be loved or will be disabled.

Pregnancy due to rape, I think the child can't be loved. It is a difficult situation because there was no consent. (Akhona, remote village)

Support could be afforded to the rape victim because they [the family] hate the act. Making matters worse is impregnating their daughter, whose child will grow in the family. They will hate the baby. (Thato, rural town)

They [women who are pregnant because of rape] should go to the clinic as early as possible because they won't be able to live with the child. She won't love the child since she did not want one, but it was because of rape. (Aphelele, commercial farming area)

A child who is a result of rape becomes disabled. You give birth to a disabled child because he/she is not planned. (Funeka, remote village)

These participants indicated that the woman and the family will 'hate' the child. Funeka mistakenly indicated that a child born of a rape would be disabled.

Another justification centred on the idea that a father should always be known, which rapists may not be.

> In that kind of situation, I would not like it [the pregnancy] at all. I wouldn't support it because we wouldn't even know who the father of the child is … It is important for a child to know their father. So, imagine when that mother has to tell the child that no, they are a result of rape. It won't sit well with the child, and they might end up doing something drastic like taking their life. (Esona, rural town)
>
> Yes, they have to accept the situation [decision to abort] because she doesn't know who raped her. No one would want to keep such a child. I would also abort. (Bongezwa, commercial farming area)
>
> No, that [a child with an unknown father] can never be right. We cannot keep a baby who has no father, a child from a rape. It could not be right with me too. (Yanela, commercial farming area)

The spectre of the fatherless child looms large here. Not knowing the father is seen as a terrible burden to the woman and the child. However, it is only rape by a stranger that is considered severe enough to warrant an abortion. If a woman is raped by someone she knows, abortion is less acceptable.

A further justification was the trauma of the rape and the child being a reminder of the event.

> Not very easy, not very easy at all. Most people think abortion straight away because it all comes as a reminder that maybe you can have this anger when you see that baby. Yes, it is your baby, but you probably have flashbacks about that day. When you see the child's face, you see the perpetrator's face. So, someone thinks, 'Ey, I don't have an option, but I tried.' They abort the child because it will be a reminder [of] how [the child] got here. (Andisiwe, rural town)
>
> On the contrary, [suggesting] that she keeps the child [means she will] feel traumatised for the rest of her life because she will

always remember how her child was born. (Simbongile, rural town)

If I was raped, I will not keep the baby because this will be a constant reminder which will open wounds that my baby is a product of rape. *He was not conceived in the normal way.* (Ziyanda, commercial farming area)

Here the participants draw on psychological narratives of trauma (flashbacks, memories, feelings of anger) to add weight to the legitimacy of rape as a reason for abortion.

Nevertheless, several participants argued that a rape victim should not abort or that families would convince her not to terminate the pregnancy.

In that situation [rape], when a woman is already pregnant, they do not do anything here. Children who grow up in the rural areas – their parents convince them to keep the baby. (Akhona, remote village)

Ehh ... they may advise her not to abort the child because she didn't choose to get pregnant. She fell pregnant because of rape. (Aphiwe, remote village)

They will advise them to abort the child, but some families insist on keeping the child even though the experience was painful. But they feel they have no choice but to keep the child. (Yamkela, rural town)

They look at you badly in that circumstance [aborting due to rape] as well because the circumstance is irrelevant, [even if] your pregnancy is not of your own will or doing. (Fezeka, remote village)

I would have no choice but to accept the pregnancy because I am already pregnant. I might not even know the person who raped me, so I would just have to accept. (Khanyiswa, remote village)

It won't sit well with them because even if you are raped, you shouldn't take out what happened on the baby. (Mpendulo, rural town)

> I don't think anyone can do something about it besides accepting the baby because the deed has been done. There is nothing they can do to undo it. (Linda, commercial farming area)

Three arguments are noteworthy here. The first is that as the conception was forced on the woman, she is not to blame (as she would be should there be conception outside of marriage). The second is the question of acceptance. In a pronatalist community where childbearing is an expected function of women, conception by rape, while regrettable, must be endured. The third is that the baby should not be affected despite the pregnancy resulting from rape. In other words, the sanctity of foetal life trumps the trauma of rape.

In the rural town, services to mitigate the traumatic effects of rape were said to be available; thus, abortion is unnecessary.

> When the child is born out of rape, the parents of the girl go to social workers. The social workers will make a plan. The child [the one carrying the baby] who has been raped and the parents will be put into counselling to show them that it is not the end for the child [the one carrying the baby]. The baby who is conceived from the rape will also get introduced to the social worker and get counselling so that they can also live a good life. (Nasipi, rural town)

> On the other side, I would say they must keep the baby and just take them to an adoption place [so that] at the end of the day they won't constantly wonder who the father of the child is. Even though that child could've been something in life, a teacher maybe. (Ntobeko, rural town)

Counselling and adoption are seen here as remedies to the problems of rape and children born from rape.

Some respondents said that the community would judge a rape victim. Their comments evoked what are known as 'rape myths', through which the blame for rape is shifted from perpetrators to victims.[18]

The whole community judges you, and all your actions are attributed to the fact that you got raped. (Fezeka, remote village)

Some of them even say, 'That person has been raped and so we do not want anything to do with them.' (Thulani, commercial farming area)

They do not view her in a negative way, but there are two things that they would say or ask. Firstly, why was it that she got raped in the first place? What was she wearing? And the community always has something to say. So, if she was wearing something short or something that is body revealing, then they will put the blame on her ... But you find out some parents allow their children to go out wearing things that are body revealing and some parents buy those [things], and as a result once she got raped the community will point fingers to those who allow their children to wear such clothes. Therefore, the community will then say the parents are to blame for their children being raped and getting pregnant. (Bulelani, rural town)

It becomes difficult because some will believe that you were raped, and some will not believe that you were raped, as if you asked for it. So, there are those who are on your side and those who are not. (Bongiwe, rural town)

I do not know because mostly people here are careles. Rape cases do happen, but there [are instances of] consent between the two. It happens in forests, roads, and when a person has been caught, she accuses the partner of raping her whereas they have agreed, and it is not taken seriously and dissipates in the thin air. (Buyiswa, commercial farming area)

Fezeka uses the passive form ('you got raped') instead of the active form ('he raped her') to describe rape. This way of describing rape dovetails with other rape myths – women get raped because of the clothes they wear, women ask for rape and women make rape up. Bulelani indicates how shifting the blame to the victim may include blaming her parents or family for allowing her to act in ways that attract rape. This would be termed stigma by association, addressed in the following chapter.

ATTITUDES TOWARDS PREGNANCY AMONG TEENAGERS, AND ABORTION

According to participants across the three sites, pregnancy among teenagers is generally viewed negatively. Issue is taken with the fact that pregnant teenagers might not complete school and that the teenager's parents or grandparents may have to care for the child. These kinds of attitudes to early reproduction are not unusual in South Africa.[19]

> Agreements or plans to have babies between younger couples or children do not make sense because they both need to finish school, grow and work, and then make plans to have children. (Fezeka, remote village)
>
> When she is not married and is a school learner, the parents get disappointed. I think even an outsider parent gets disappointed because when you are a parent, you are not only a parent in your house, but you are a parent even out there, and you know her future can become bleak. She can stop going to school regularly. Maybe the mother may not allow her to keep the baby or [may] want her to raise the baby, and then she will get behind at school. (Amanda, rural town)
>
> Wow! That [early reproduction] will be a bad thing. For a school-going child to get pregnant is a disgrace. That will delay the female partner in her studies, whereas there will be no disruption on the side of the boy's studies. Parents, once being made aware of the situation, tend to let their child give birth. Thereafter, they look after the baby and let the mother return to school. (Thato, rural town)
>
> I know the responsibility of giving birth to a child because when that child is sick, they are dependent on me, as the grandparent. I

had a vision of my child studying and making it in life. Now they cut those plans with having a child. (Kuhle, remote village)

These extracts illustrate the commonly held view concerning the correct timing of reproduction – after schooling is complete and after marriage. To rupture this socially sanctioned order of reproduction results in 'disappointment' and 'disgrace'. Amanda refers to what is called social parenting, whereby adult members of a community share parenting responsibility for children who are not their biological offspring. Thato points to the gendered dimension of early reproduction (negative repercussions for the young woman but not her conception partner), while Kuhle speaks to personal experience in relation to her child giving birth.

Besides the moral reprobation of early pregnancies ('disgrace'), the participants speak about the disruption of schooling, not 'making it in life', or having a 'bleak' future. These consequences have been debated extensively in the literature on teenage pregnancy.[20] Two issues are worth noting. First, well-designed comparative research shows very few differences in the long term health, economic or social consequences of reproduction below or above the age of 20 among women of the same socio-economic status.[21] Second, pregnancy and child rearing tend to disrupt women's lives, whether they are at school or working (outside the home). The support of workplaces in relation to pregnancy and childbirth (a hard-won victory by the women's movement) should be extended to schools, as outlined by Robert Morrell et al.[22]

Participants indicated that young women who conceive are subjected to gossip.

The community gossip about people so much. It's as if the child was not brought up the right way, or they don't follow their parents' teachings or the child is sleeping around – although maybe it was her first time having sex, and she was unfortunate and got pregnant. So she is always stigmatised as if she is always doing wrong. (Bongiwe, rural town)

People will keep talking always, and you can't help that. When a father of the baby says he wants the baby, people will not get involved. They will just keep talking, and the couple will just have to ignore them. (Ziyanda, commercial farming area)

The community judges. People judge. For example, young children get pregnant, and we tend to judge them a lot. We even call them names ... Some teenagers decide to have an abortion because they start thinking of various things – like what the community will say, what their parents will say – so they terminate. (Mpendulo, rural town)

Yes, we do not want too many pregnancies coming from young couples, but that does not mean that we must force them to have abortions just because they are too young. (Simbongile, rural town)

Here participants admit to young people being the subject of gossip and judgement (or stigma; see the following chapter). Some connect this kind of stigma to young people deciding – or being coerced – to terminate their pregnancy.

Participants indicated that the parents of a pregnant teenager, especially the mother, are likely to make the decision whether to abort. If the teenager's parents are willing and able to look after the child, she will not abort, but if not, or if the parents are concerned about their or their daughter's reputation, they would take her to the hospital to have an abortion. This obviously contradicts the CTOP Act, in which minors are empowered to make their own decisions regarding the outcome of a pregnancy.

It is bad [abortion], but some parents do such things. They would see that the child is still young and will bring the reputation of the family into disrepute and be the laughingstock of the village. (Thato, rural town)

In the case of abortion, the parent makes the decision. When the child doesn't have a parent, if they were raised by their grand-

mother, the grandmother makes the decision. Most of these children go to school in the location or in Port Elizabeth, and because
the parent does not want to be humiliated, they secretly abort
the child and [then] we notice the child is no longer pregnant.
(Athenkosi, commercial farming area)

Here the participants speak to stigma being extended to the young
person's family. This is stigma by association, in which people close to the
stigmatised person – often family members – are also discredited. John
Pryor et al. refer to this as 'the infection of bad company'.[23] This kind of
familial stigma by association could, according to participants, lead to
families coercing young people into an abortion.

CONCLUSION

As is the case in other parts of South Africa, communities in these
rural sites generally have negative attitudes towards abortion. Abortion
is viewed as 'not right' – an act of murder, potentially of someone who
would have had a bright future – and as leading to psychological damage
and physical health problems, particularly infertility. Such opposition was not, however, seamless. Participants indicated that there are
differing views within communities. Provisional acceptance based on
the circumstances was espoused, particularly in the cases of poverty, violence, rape and unwed pregnant women. Tolerance and non-judgemental
attitudes were argued for in such cases.

Non-judgementalism was viewed as automatic in cases of rape, for
which support and compassion should be forthcoming. Justifications
for abortion in these circumstances centred on the trauma from the
rape (including the child serving as a reminder of the act) and the fact
that the father is (probably) not known. Once again, however, these
understandings were not seamless. Rape was sometimes seen as rescuing
the woman from accusations of conceiving out of wedlock. And, despite
the pregnancy being the result of rape, community members may argue

that the child is precious and the woman is fulfilling a mothering role. Some participants drew on rape myths to suggest that the woman was responsible for the rape and should therefore live with the consequences.

Participants spoke to a double bind, discussed by Catriona Macleod in a previous publication, in which abortion is viewed as socially unacceptable but so too is teenage pregnancy.[24] According to our study participants, acceptable reproduction occurs after schooling is complete and within wedlock. Participants acknowledged that these norms and the gossip that follows early pregnancies might lead young women to terminate their pregnancies. Such stigma extends to the families, who must decide whether they will care for the child if born.

Extracts featured in this chapter spoke to community judgements and gossip. In these actions, community members ascribe negative characteristics to the women. This process is theorised in stigma research, which we turn to in the next chapter.

4

'And the Story Spread': Abortion Stigma in Rural South Africa

There was a girl who had an abortion, and the news got out that she had an abortion because someone who worked at the local hospital leaked the information without any consent. As [the girl] told me, she was also seen by someone who is familiar to her when she went into that room, so they suspected that she might have been going to get an abortion. To that person's knowledge, it was not the girl's first abortion but her third. After that, a lot of people spoke about her, and it became very well known that she had an abortion. It got so bad that she ended up leaving the village because it affected her so much. She even lost a lot of weight. She is no longer around here. (Ntobeko, rural town)

In the quote above, a participant from our study outlines how news of a girl who had an abortion led to much gossip and negativity. This negativity attached to the person herself rather than the abortion, leading to various consequences for the young woman, including loss of weight and her leaving the village. This extract illustrates the social dynamics of stigmatising interactions.

Several extracts in previous chapters have pointed to stigmatising actions. Indeed, along with structural barriers to abortions, stigma surfaced as a key issue in participants' talk about accessing abortion services. We start this chapter by outlining key conceptual developments around abortion stigma. We then discuss the abortion stigma evident in our data. We examine interview extracts pointing to experienced, perceived and internalised stigma and reports of how women manage stigma.

CONCEPTUALISING ABORTION STIGMA

A few authors have focused on conceptualising abortion stigma,[1] and some methodological tools have been produced to measure it.[2] Anuradha Kumar et al., whose definition is often used, view abortion stigma as 'a negative attribute ascribed to women who seek to terminate a pregnancy that marks them, internally or externally, as inferior to ideals of womanhood'.[3]

Most scholars who approach the topic of stigma draw on Erving Goffman's 1963 pioneering work to understand or explain the mechanics of stigma.[4] Goffman described stigma as an attribute held by certain people that is discrediting and leads to a 'spoiled identity'. These attributes could include anything from bodily deformities, behaviour, health issues and race to economic status. Goffman outlined three major types of stigma:

1. 'abominations of the body', indicating physical deformities;
2. 'blemishes of individual character', pointing to decision making, behaviour or personality traits of individuals; and
3. 'tribal stigma', or characteristics 'that can be transmitted through lineages', such as race, nation, religion, and so on.[5]

Abortion stigma is generally described as falling within 'blemishes of individual character' in that it can be seen as an act that stains a person's moral character or as an individual failure of womanhood. Kate Cockrill and Adina Nack identify tribal stigma as a possible way in which abortion stigma can be explained since there are ideal women 'tribes': the 'good girls/wives/mothers' tribe and the 'bad girls and fallen women' tribe.[6]

Stigma rests on 'stigma theories' – the ideologies or rationalisations constructed to explain the inferiority or dangerousness of the individual with the stigmatised attribute. These theories justify women's exclusion from society. For instance, religious interpretations of when the soul enters the foetus, and with it the rationalisation of abortion as murder, act as stigma theory.[7] Other abortion stigma theories involve norms regarding ideal womanhood. These usually include (1) assumptions that women will desire and fulfil childbearing[8] (as indicated by one of our participants: 'I think everyone has a wish to have children so that they can see that they are fertile' [Athule, rural town]); (2) questions of the legality of the abortion procedure, with illegal abortions attracting criminal implications; and (3) views of the procedure as disgusting (due to unsafe abortion practices).[9]

Bruce Link and Jo Phelan explain stigma as a tool to perpetuate the status quo.[10] They argue that the production of stigma is a social process that uses cultural, economic and political power relations to maintain the current state of affairs. The process evolves in stages. The first stage involves the demarcation of difference: those who engage in the stigmatised activity (in this case, abortion) are somehow different from the norm (here, as indicated above, the norms of womanhood). This requires significant denial of the regularity with which abortion occurs.

Indeed, singling out women who have undergone an abortion as aberrant is disputed by data showing that abortion is in fact a common gynaecological procedure. An average of 73.3 million induced abortions occur worldwide each year.[11] The Guttmacher Institute estimates that 24% of pregnancies in southern Africa end in abortion, which indicates that abortion is by no means a rare occurrence.[12] However, the demarcation of difference produces a 'mutually reinforcing cycle of silence,'[13] supporting the belief that abortion is rare. This denial of the regularity of abortion is a requirement for abortion stigma to fashion itself in the first place *and* to sustain itself. If abortion is considered an everyday occurrence, the deviant label attached to people who have had an abortion will collapse; a stigmatised action cannot be the norm.

Link and Phelan's second stage requires the created category – women who undergo abortions – to be linked to undesirable characteristics.[14] In previous chapters, we presented extracts in which our participants either ascribed or indicated that community members ascribed the following characteristics to women who undergo an abortion: murderer, sinner, robber of children's bright futures, adulteress, psychologically unstable, irresponsible in risking infertility (and therefore the ability to fulfil their mothering roles) and in risking death. As Carole Joffe points out, the abundance of illegal abortion providers and the use of unsafe home-made abortifacients may influence how abortion is perceived in these communities, particularly in relation to infertility and death.[15] Nevertheless, as noted in the previous chapter, these attitudes about abortion are common in South Africa, even when safe, legal abortion is being considered.[16]

The third stage in the stigma process is where 'them' and 'us' are created based on the ascribed undesirable characteristics. For example, the 'murderers' are 'them' [people having abortions], while 'we' are good people who preserve foetal life. Through this dichotomy, the cycle of silence (about the regularity of abortion as a gynaecological procedure) is confirmed and reinforces itself because, out of fear of associated stigma, people become unwilling to support women who have abortions.

The final stage is discrimination. This may take various forms. For example, in the USA, anti-abortion activists engage in such activities as picketing at abortion clinics, harassment, stalking and vandalism.[17] These organised anti-abortion groups have exported their ideas and tactics to countries such as South Africa by funding the spread of misinformation on abortion. For example, 'pregnancy crisis centres' based on North American models have been set up. When women wanting an abortion come to these centres, staff employ misinformation and fear tactics to try to convince them not to have the procedure.[18] Anti-abortionists have also been found inside South Africa's public hospitals, where they have presented themselves as legitimate abortion counsellors. Since they are willing to provide their pre-abortion 'counselling' for free, hospital managers have jumped at the opportunity to provide these services without scrutinising the credentials or ideologies of these so-called counsellors.[19]

STIGMA IN OUR DATA

Kristin Shellenberg and Amy Tsui divide stigma into three domains: perceived, experienced and internalised.[20] Perceived stigma refers to the stigma a woman believes she will experience after having an abortion. Experienced stigma includes all actual experiences of stigma. Internalised stigma is an internalisation of the views of those who would stigmatise abortion. The results of internalised stigma are usually guilt, shame, anxiety and feeling the need to keep secret the fact that one has had an abortion. In the following, we outline findings regarding experienced, perceived and internalised stigma evident in our data

Experienced stigma

Consistent with other studies,[21] our participants did not provide many descriptions of actual experiences of stigma; reports of perceived stigma were more frequent.

Few participants spoke directly about their own abortion experiences. However, those who did talked about instances where the abortion was made known without their consent.

> When I got there, the clerk who gave me my folder read the letter first. It is a procedure to read the letter first before they could assist so that they know where to refer you to, which facility around the hospital. She found out I wanted to do abortion. There was a line behind me full of people. Then she shouted: 'You were supposed to

stand in a line! You are here for an abortion! Even if the ambulance brought you, you are supposed to stand in a line!' (Bongiwe, rural town)

Bongiwe relates how, without her consent, the clinic, which was 'full of people', was made aware that she was presenting for an abortion. Although in this quote she does not refer directly to the consequences, the implication is clear. Many people knew why she was at the clinic and would judge her for having an abortion.

Study participants were asked whether they knew someone or knew of someone in their community who had had an abortion and how community members responded to the knowledge of the abortion. The quote at the beginning of this chapter speaks in clear terms of experienced stigma. Ntobeko relates a case of a woman's abortion being made public knowledge without her consent. The resultant experienced stigma was 'so bad' that it led to the woman's weight loss and her leaving the village.

Perceived stigma

Many participants spoke about how abortion would be negatively perceived, leading to much gossip and judgement on the part of the community.

> You just hear about it when you gossip with friends, or if you've done it and you tell a friend in confidence, she may tell everyone else because it is scandalous. (Gcobisa, remote village)
>
> [If you are being judged within the community,] it means you have said your secret to someone you trusted, and that person leaked it and the story spread. It happens that way. (Thato, rural town)

Here participants speak to the perception that abortion will inevitably lead to stigma. Abortion is 'scandalous' and gossiped about.

While much of the perceived stigma spoken about referred to non-distinct community members, some participants related incidents of partners stigmatising women who had undergone an abortion.

> He does not forget. Say, for example, the couple goes out some-where to have some fun. Maybe while they are there, it happens that some random guy approaches you and chats with you. He [the boyfriend] will be angered to see you chatting with other guys. He will act funny, asking you how can you talk with someone else while you are with him there. You understand? He will then bring this abortion thing up again and say it out loud in front of the public, and as a result, people will be shocked to hear that you had an abortion. However, it does not matter anymore that you guys had actually agreed together to get an abortion, because people do not know that. All they know is what they are hearing right now. Therefore, the blame or the stigma would be on you only, and the guy will not tell them that you both decided to get an abortion, so blame is always on the woman because she is the one who has terminated her pregnancy. (Bulelani, rural town)

This story illustrates Link and Phelan's argument that stigma is about retaining the status quo.[22] In this case, the status quo is the gendered relations in which a woman's actions within an intimate heterosexual relationship are monitored and regulated. In the narrative above, the woman steps outside patriarchal heterosexual relations by 'chatting' with other men. The stigmatising consequence of the partner's announcement (without providing the contextual background of joint decision making) serves to punish the woman for her transgression (chatting to other men).

In order to tap into class-based status quo power relations in relation to abortion stigma, participants were asked who would more likely be judged for having an abortion: a wealthy woman or a poor woman. This question elicited some understanding of the dynamics of class in the areas under study. While there was a relatively equal distribution between those who reported that rich women would be more judged than poor women and those who reported that poor women would be more judged than rich women, the explanations given as to why rich women might not get judged elucidated how class-based power relations might operate in the community.

> The situation may be that person who is rich, you'll find that some people judge her … while you find that maybe other people love her because they know that maybe she is rich. They don't bad-mouth her, because they know that maybe that person has money. But you find that when maybe it's a person who doesn't have money, people look down on her in the community and bad-mouth her. (Amahle, rural town)
>
> They will normally be intimidated because the lady might get them arrested because she can afford lawyers. (Yamkela, rural town)
>
> They will gossip about the poor one, and others will somehow say she did it because of her situation. No one wants to be on the bad side of a rich person, so they will not even gossip about her. (Athule, rural town)
>
> Because they feel that if they can go to the rich woman's house and talk about what the poor woman did, the rich woman would be able to give them something, but with the poor woman, since she doesn't have anything, they won't benefit from her. (Thulani, commercial farming area)

These extracts portray in stark terms the power relations that play out around class. According to these participants, wealthier women who terminate a pregnancy will be spared judgement as community members fear intimidation or welcome the possibility of currying favour with a person with resources.

Although rich women are slightly less likely to be openly judged for having had an abortion, they were criticised since they are able to care for a child financially. This same logic is, for the most part, what lets poor or unemployed women off the hook for having had an abortion.

> The wealthy one is the one who planned the pregnancy and can take care of the child. She has money. She works and all that. The other one is doing the right thing to abort because she has no money. (Khethiwe, remote village)
>
> They will ask questions because they will wonder why they [the wealthy person] had an abortion because [she has] the money to raise a child. Maybe they might understand the poor one and say she wouldn't be able to raise a child. (Mpendulo, rural town)
>
> The one who is not struggling is not supposed to have abortion. The one who is struggling knows her situation, so she doesn't want to have a child that will also struggle. So she decides on abortion, or maybe the boyfriend is denying [paternity]. (Bongezwa, commercial farming area)

The consequences of poverty are keenly felt by members of the resource-poor areas where we conducted this research. This is reflected in the above extracts in which poverty is seen as a completely legitimate reason to terminate a pregnancy. On the other hand, wealthy women work, have money, do not struggle, plan the pregnancy and 'can take care of the child'.

Although poverty was generally seen as an acceptable reason to terminate a pregnancy, some participants indicated that it did not always exempt women from judgement.

> She is not allowed to get an abortion. A person who is poor and married. (Nasipi, rural town)
>
> Some will say she was right because she had no way of raising the child and looking after it. Some will say she could have kept it, and a plan would have come along. You hear? (Anelisa, commercial farming area)

We make sure we report them. They are the ones that should be arrested. Even the poor one. Why did they make a child [just] to have an abortion? They must give birth to them. They will just have to use the R400 grant money and buy Huggies and clothes from Pep. (Aphelele, commercial farming area)

They [the community] feel hurt because they feel that had the person spoken up, [she] would have been helped. They would have seen what they could do to assist her with her child. (Boipelo, commercial farming area)

Nasipi's statement illustrates how marital status trumps poverty. If the woman is married, poverty is not an excuse for an abortion. Participants Anelisa, Aphelele and Boipelo speak to possible solutions to poverty in relation to childbearing: making a plan, using the child-support grant money and asking the community for support. The logic is that there is no reason to terminate the pregnancy if there are solutions.

Some respondents indicated that when community members make assumptions about the reasons for an abortion, they do not factor poverty into the equation.

They do not take that into consideration [that you were too poor to have a child]. They just assume that if you want an abortion while you are in a relationship, then you must have been cheating on your partner or that you are sick with something like HIV and you do not want to give birth to a child that is HIV-positive. People just tend to make assumptions along those lines. (Ntobeko, rural town)

Rich or not, there is no difference. (Simbongile, rural town)

Despite financial standing, we did the same thing [abort], so our judgement will be the same. (Lwandisa, commercial farming area)

In these extracts, participants indicate that poverty is not factored into judgements regarding abortion. Indeed, other factors such as infidelity or living with HIV are considered more likely reasons for obtaining an abortion. Here, not only is abortion stigmatised, but so is the reason – infidelity or HIV-positive status. Given the pervasiveness of poverty in the areas in which we collected our data, it is difficult to single out poverty for stigmatisation.

Participants reported how stigma does not diminish over time but is maintained and reinforced.

> It [the abortion] will pass momentarily but will remain a stigma. The stigma can last up to ten years. Let's say by then the girl has finished her studies, is self-sufficient, having her own car, but it will remain that she once aborted. At times, whenever she is playing with our kids, we will be reminded that she aborted her own. It does not go away at all; it has consequences from time to time. (Thato, rural town)

> People in the community always have something to say, and abortion to them is not a good thing. Because if your child or a child from next door has had an abortion, she will always have stigma on her. People will always remind you that your child has had an abortion, and wherever she is going, even if she has changed or she is educated or working, you will find that people are still putting that abortion tag on her. Therefore, it remains as stigma even if you have moved on with life and you have left the past in the past. But people in the community always judge you by the actions of your past. Hence, abortion becomes a stigma. (Bulelani, rural town)

These participants indicated that the stigma from abortion does not diminish; rather, 'it will remain'; 'she will always have stigma on her'. Reminders such as playing with children or people 'still putting that abortion tag on her' assist in this process. Stigma is said to attach itself not only to the woman but also to her family (associated stigma) – Bulelani indicates that 'people will always remind you [the parent] that your child has had an abortion'.

Internalised stigma

In our research, we purposefully did not ask people to relay personal experiences of abortion. There are two reasons for this. The first is a sensitivity to the lack of support for those who have undergone an abortion and an awareness of the possible retraumatisation that discussing abortion directly may bring about. The second is that we were interested in community responses to abortion and hypothetical abortion service preferences (as outlined in the DCE methodology). Nevertheless, participants did bring up their personal experiences, and some referred to the internalised stigma that resulted.

> Just like me. I had an abortion in 2003, but there are people who still remind me of that. (Bongiwe, rural town)
>
> There is a person I know that had an abortion, and she found it too difficult to stay here. The burden was too much. She ended up being sent away. She left to stay in another place. (Amahle, rural town)

Bongiwe speaks to the longevity of abortion stigma. Despite having procured an abortion over 15 years ago (at the time of data collection), people in her community still remind her of it. Abortion, she suggests, is not a forgettable occurrence. Like Ntobeko in the quote at the beginning of the chapter, Amahle does not speak from personal experience but speaks about a person who internalised stigma to the extent that it affected her physiological health ('lost a lot of weight') and drove her out of the village.

REPORTS OF STIGMA MANAGEMENT

Given the pervasive character of abortion stigma, it is foreseeable that women will attempt to manage or diminish stigma. Cockrill and Nack identified a variety of individual stigma-management strategies.[23] The first involves the management of the damaged self. Women managing the damaged self will make excuses for their decision to abort, or they will justify it; others will transfer all or some of the blame to others or 'appeal to higher loyalties'[24] such as to their partner and other children. Another strategy is that of maintaining a good reputation, which mainly involves being secretive or fabricating a cover story in case the pregnancy was known about before the abortion. Finally, there is the strategy of managing the damaged reputation. This might involve condemning those who hold an anti-abortion stance and normalising the abortion experience.

Unlike physical deformities, the experience of having an abortion can, for the most part, be hidden.[25] As a result, avoiding abortion stigma hinges a great deal on concealment or maintaining a good reputation. The dominant strategy of concealment spoken about by our participants was to go to an abortion clinic that is not close by or to perform the abortion illegally.

> She can go far. For example, our village is quite a distance from Mthatha. A person might go to Mthatha and say that they are going to town, or someone with a relative in Mthatha can go there, terminate the pregnancy and stay there, and come back when they are all right. We will not know that. (Lindelwa, remote village)
>
> Yes, if I want to hide, I would go far away, and I would rather pay a lot of money if it is about hiding. (Ziyanda, commercial farming area)
>
> At the hospitals, they feel like they are not protected from some nurses who might go around speaking about them … I have heard that it is because people are avoiding being spoken about badly due to the lack of confidentiality at the hospitals. So they choose to go elsewhere [to have an abortion]. (Ntobeko, rural town)
>
> Fear of people's perception is what normally compels most women to pay a lot of money to go far for abortions. (Simbongile, rural town)
>
> So, I think people choose to go to these places they see on posters around town [illegal abortion providers] most of the time because they don't want anyone to know. (Bongiwe, rural town)

> I would say if they do not have any other way, they must do it the traditional way, like how I have explained that people do it by combining different things. Because in this case, they do not want people to know and going to the hospital will be a problem. Maybe they will come across someone who knows their mother or someone who will say, 'I saw so and so at the hospital', whereas her family didn't know she went there. (Esona, rural town)

Here participants talk about women travelling, with a made-up story, to a distant facility or going to illegal or traditional providers. These concealment strategies, however, come with costs. The expense of travel can sometimes be considerably more than the procedure would cost in a private or illegal facility. In one of our research areas, a trip to the nearest city with a hospital costs R800. Depending on how far the village is from this city, accommodation and subsistence costs would also need to be included. Sometimes multiple visits are required. Illegal or traditional abortions may also be unsafe and incur significant health costs.

Where a woman has managed not to be seen going to an abortion clinic, participants also suggested that they should remain tight-lipped over the abortion.

> For instance, when it is still small and unnoticeable, and I am the only one who knows about it … when I leave home, I'd walk alone, and I would go alone to see a doctor and sort this thing out alone. If ever there is someone else close and I tell them, they might tell others here in the township, so it is better that I walk alone. (Yanela, commercial farming area)

The majority of these strategies fall under Cockrill and Nack's blueprint of maintaining a good reputation,[26] specifically the acts of being secretive and fabricating a cover story.

In the case of second-trimester abortions, which are relatively common in South Africa, concealment is more difficult. Participants often mentioned the possibility that people will notice a difference in body size.

> [Talking about second-trimester abortion] Without a doubt, they will start gossiping about her. I mean, her pregnancy would have already been showing, so she will be the talk of the town because they will say she has killed her baby. (Azole, rural town)
>
> The one who terminated the pregnancy and was already showing – the community will not let her rest because everyone saw her. Then the other one, because she was not showing, people will not know unless she tells people that she aborted the pregnancy because she wanted to. Even then, the people will still give her trouble. (Bongiwe, rural town)

Given the gossip mentioned above, it was not surprising that our data show the extreme importance of maintaining confidentiality during and after an abortion. Our participants, very few of whom had had an abortion or were even pro abortion, almost all reiterated that the most important aspects of accessing abortion and the decision-making process (including choosing the facility) were related to the need to be able to conceal the fact that you are having an abortion.

Concealment is not enabled through free-standing abortion clinics in villages or small towns. Participants indicated that these would be avoided entirely in case someone happened to see them go into the building. Indeed, free-standing abortion clinics were deemed the least preferred option in our DCE study (see chapter 6). Clinics with open waiting rooms where people could come and go were also considered too risky.

> It's important [that the abortion facility] be a safe place. I must not be sitting and waiting to abort in an open room. It must be a safe place, and a trustworthy person must do this. It can't be a place where suddenly the door is opened, passers-by are looking in the window to see what I was doing. (Andisiwe, rural town)

> At this clinic, everyone will know you aborted … because at the clinics we use, it's already obvious to the people what you are going to do when you enter a certain room. (Sinoxolo, commercial farming area)

Here participants emphasise the importance of 'safety', which includes not being seen by others and others not knowing why you are presenting at the clinic.

While structural issues (how the clinic is named – i.e., not as an abortion clinic – and privacy) were seen as important for concealment, the factor spoken about repeatedly was service providers breaking confidentiality. This was particularly evident in the rural town, where several participants mentioned that the town clinic must be avoided if you want to do an HIV test or have any other potentially gossip-worthy health concern.

> What happens is that we are of this village, we are scared to use our own clinic because news travels fast. What people fear the most is getting tested [for HIV] because they say people will gossip about your results. People choose to go to other clinics like [in the next village], but there is no difference … Other people go as far as using taxis to go to the clinics only because they are avoiding the one [here], and they do not want to be tested there. (Athule, rural town)
>
> Most of the people who were using that clinic have their secrets known by the villagers. (Buyiswa, commercial farming area)
>
> If there was a clinic, they would go to the clinic. But the nurses at the clinic would be a member of this community, and she could help you, but you have the fear that they will speak of your problems. [It would be great] if you felt safe with the fact that they will not disclose your problem to other people so that you will not be humiliated. (Gcobisa, remote village)

The unauthorised disclosure of confidential health information by doctors and nurses is a risk that increases in rural areas where communities are close-knit and little anonymity exists. These participants speak of breaches of confidentiality almost as a given. To avoid this and to ensure the concealment of the abortion, women may travel great distances to visit clinics outside of their area. Once the abortion is known, however, other concealment strategies are needed – as in the case of the person who 'ended up leaving the village because it affected her so much' (cited at the beginning of the chapter).

The approach of coping with stigma *through managing a damaged reputation* did not appear much in the data. This strategy involves condemning those who hold an anti-abortion stance and normalising the abortion experience. Khethiwe was an outlier in this regard.

> When I come to a clinic here, am I scared of being caught? When I'm doing this, am I thinking of being caught? Am I doing it as a secret? I honestly wouldn't be afraid of anything, and after that, I would go back home. I wouldn't go far when the clinic is here to do the abortion. Let me just say I wouldn't hide anything. Because when I am hiding it, I would have to go to [closest city]. I would have had my reasons that made me do it. I wouldn't just get an abortion for no reason. (Khethiwe, remote village)

Here the participant eschews secrecy. She argues that having 'my reasons' should be sufficient and that fear of 'being caught' should play no role in responses to abortion. She relates the costs of managing stigma through concealment – you have to travel far.

Another way in which gossip spreads is through someone you told something to. Participants were asked whether they thought a woman who had an abortion would tell anyone, whether it be family, friends or other community members. The answers were predominantly no.

> There is no support that females who have terminated get in the community. A person is in it by themselves. They thought of it alone and they do it alone without being seen. (Kuhle, remote village)

The women do not get any support when they go get an abortion. The person gets stigma and is not loved by the community. (Nasipi, rural town)

I would need family supports the most. You have to be selective when talking to the outsiders, and you can't talk to any person about a situation like this. (Ziyanda, commercial farming area)

These extracts reveal the sad reality of stigma: 'a person is in it by themselves'. Support is not readily available.

CONCLUSION

Abortion stigma has become prominent as a topic of inquiry in scholarly and activist circles. It has been used to explain the actions of women undertaking abortions and how experienced, perceived and internalised stigma work within communities to retain the status quo. While knowledge of abortion laws and practices was not low among our participants, and public health abortion services were generally deemed safe, the idea persists that women who terminate pregnancies are tainted in various ways. This has various consequences for women. They are judged, gossiped about, excluded, denounced and experience ill health. The stigmatisation of women who abort maintains a gendered status quo in which women are meant to fulfil the ideals of procreative womanhood. Such stigmatisation is not even, however, with particular class-based power relations playing themselves out in ways that protect wealthier women from the worst effects of stigma.

Stigma requires management. This speaks to the key conundrum highlighted in this book: confidentiality versus costs. Maintaining a good reputation was the stigma-management technique most spoken of in our data. This involved concealing the abortion and not confiding in anybody. Concealment consists of travelling far to obtain the service – outside of the surveillance of fellow community members – or of undergoing an illegal abortion through ingesting local abortifacients or consulting a traditional healer. Thus, maintaining a good reputation comes at a considerable cost – transport and other costs or risking health and life with a possible unsafe abortion. If confidentiality and privacy cannot be ensured within the community, then the above costs must be borne to avoid stigma, which, according to some of our participants, does not diminish with time. The conundrum of confidentiality and costs is therefore deeply embedded within the social processes that produce stigma. Ensuring confidentiality is costly. When these costs cannot be met, confidentiality is not assured, leading to stigma and the associated costs: judgement, social exclusion, a spoiled identity and possible physical harm. These costs are underpinned by understandings of womanhood, procreation and the value of children – the breaking of which results in abortion stigma.

5

Barriers to Having an Abortion in Rural South Africa

Significant barriers to accessing formal abortion services in South Africa have been highlighted in the literature. A study by Catriona Macleod and colleagues provides a summary of these barriers, among which are active dissuasion by others, including by referring healthcare providers; healthcare providers citing conscientious objection to providing services; a shortage of functioning facilities; lack of facility managers' support (resulting in poor human and physical resourcing of open clinics); women fearing breaches of confidentiality; costs; and stigma.[1] These findings are based on either national data or urban-based studies. In our study, we were interested in barriers experienced specifically by abortion seekers in rural areas.

We therefore asked our participants whether they could think of any barriers women in their community might face when deciding to have an abortion. The most prominent barrier mentioned was confidentiality:

the fear that either nurses or community members who see a woman at the clinic will share that information with others. The second most prominent barrier reported was distance to the abortion facility of choice (where the woman is not known).

These barriers represent the major conundrum highlighted in this book: confidentiality versus cost. Women take a risk in terms of confidentiality by going to a local clinic. The logical solution is to travel to a clinic where they can be guaranteed anonymity, thus reducing the risk of confidential information being made known to their family, friends or community members. But for women who do not have money for travel, there are other choices: take the risk of their abortion being known in the community (and thus take on the resultant stigma and shame), forfeit their right to an abortion, seek traditional or illegal providers, or self-induce.

Some of the other barriers reported by our participants are related to the issue of confidentiality and distance, including costs (the expense of travel) and failing to present for an abortion within the legal time limit (because of the time involved in travelling to and obtaining services from a clinic where anonymity is guaranteed). Many participants also spoke about their fear of abortion and its potential consequences as a barrier, as well as their fear of hostility towards abortion at clinics or from those they turn to for advice. Other barriers include partner attitudes, lack of support, lack of information on abortion and abortion services, and the fear of abortion being illegal. These are discussed below.

THE INABILITY TO MAINTAIN CONFIDENTIALITY IN ACCESSING AN ABORTION

Women who have an abortion are at risk of being judged by the community to such an extent that it has a detrimental effect on their right to access abortion, including forcing them to travel far even in cases where a closer facility is available. As outlined by participants, the main reason was that local clinic workers would break confidentiality, informing community members about the abortion. This has been discussed extensively in the previous chapter, but the fear of confidentiality breaches is repeated here as a barrier to abortion access.

> What influences their decision making is the issue of confidentiality. This is because if they abort at the local clinic, the community will know through social networks. This will affect the woman negatively. Even if people are just chatting, she will be insecure, thinking that they are discussing her abortion. (Bamanye, rural town)
>
> She can go to the place maybe that's far. It depends on her how she wants to do it. She can go to the place that's far because sometimes you come to realise that you don't want to go to the place where you are known. Your news will spread, people talking, so maybe [go to] a place where you are not known ... where you know it will be confidential. (Amahle, rural town)

Participants indicate that 'the community will know' and 'news will spread'. These kinds of stories of breaches of confidentiality are not isolated incidents and have been recorded in other research in South Africa.[2]

Local nurses breaking their oath of confidentiality seems to be an ongoing issue in one of our research sites, with multiple participants alluding to this fact. The intimate nature of the clinics also contributes to breaches of confidentiality.

> There are challenges. For example, if my sister does not have a phone, I am the one who is called when she is needed, and the personnel from that clinic do not have a secret. They tell over the phone the reason for their call, and if they do not get me, they phone another and divulge the reason for their call. Most of the people who were using that clinic have their secrets known by the villagers. (Buyiswa, commercial farming area)

It will depend [on] where the woman wants to go. At this clinic, everyone will know you aborted, or you can choose to go where you will not be known. Because at the clinics we use, it's already obvious to the people what you're going to do when you enter a certain room. (Sinoxolo, commercial farming area)

Well, since we are known at this clinic, we are familiar with almost everyone at this clinic. You would never really trust a nurse, because a person can take your information and share it with others because we know each other here. They would probably choose a place where no one knows them. (Linda, commercial farming area)

Buyiswa outlines how breaches of confidentiality may occur in rural areas where households may share phones. Sinoxolo and Linda suggest that it is not only nurses breaching confidentiality but also the obviousness within the clinic of people's presenting problems that exposes the pregnant woman's situation.

DISTANCE AND COSTS

An often-quoted barrier to accessing an abortion was the distance that women needed to travel for the service. Hospitals are usually in the nearest city or large town, but even clinics are sometimes difficult to access. The issue of distance was especially prominent in the remote village. Distance is connected to the question of costs. Travel is expensive and distant travel requires accommodation. Since abortions are free in public hospitals, costs are directly related to the distance travelled (including the possible need for accommodation).

It is difficult because from our community ... to the clinic is far. We travel for a day. If you leave your house at 10 am, you will get back home around 4 pm. The clinic is across a river, so we use small boats to get to the clinic. There is someone who helps us to cross the river. Sometimes we wait by the river and wait for the person to drive the boat to the other side, where there is a clinic. (Akhona, remote village)

[Nearest city] is far away. You pass two towns before you get there. Even our own town is far from us because when you go to our town the transport fare is R40 and the return is R80. I'm not too sure how much it is when you go to [second-nearest town]. [Nearest city] is further from [second-nearest town]. (Lindelwa, remote village)

It [distance as a barrier] is important because sometimes you must travel. If you go to that place, you need to have money. (Amahle, rural town)

As I said, people don't know about terminations here, so no one has terminated because services like that are out of reach. Even if you think about it, it won't happen because it is not available even in [nearby town], which is far! Rather you just keep your baby, you see. (Lwandisa, commercial farming area)

The participants speak here to direct costs, particularly taxi fees, and indirect costs. Getting to a clinic takes a long time, interfering with other potential activities, such as household, caregiving or money-generating activities. Because of the topography surrounding the remote village, there is no direct road access to the clinic. Instead, people must walk and be rowed across the river in small crafts.

In a study by Naomi Lince-Deroche et al., women were found to have incurred a median cost of R190 for an abortion, which usually required two facility visits.[3] Many had to pay for transportation, a pregnancy test, sanitary pads and pain medication. Reserving family resources for transport can be extremely difficult or impossible in rural areas, where people are mostly unemployed and generally depend for their livelihood on subsistence or small-scale farming, small businesses, social grants or stipends sent by relatives working elsewhere.

Even if rural pregnant people can travel to hospitals in other locations for an abortion, there is no guarantee that they will be served on the day they visit the hospital. This may be due to the oversubscribed nature of the public healthcare system. The requirement to queue when one gets to the clinic or hospital has been normalised.

> They wait. It does not matter how long, because they want to be assisted. (Esihle, remote village)
>
> It gets full … you will get there and queue. Something you do for yourself is to wake up early and make sure you are first or second. (Andisiwe, rural town)
>
> Sometimes a person is determined to abort at any cost and opts for a short cut because at the hospital it won't be done immediately. (Bamanye, rural town)

Participants speak here of inevitable waiting and queuing. This is exacerbated if multiple visits are required. The difficulty of women being sent from one facility to another or being told to return on a different day has been reported in the literature.[4] Women may thus need to make another trip. Indeed, research has shown that some women wait a long time (up to three weeks) before obtaining the abortion they requested.[5]

The costs of procuring an abortion, even where the service is free of charge, are a potential factor in presenting late for an abortion. If they or their families do not have the resources, pregnant people may delay accessing the service as they must save enough money first.[6] We turn to this issue in the next section.

Distance and costs are interlinked with the dearth of functioning facilities, especially in rural areas. As Jane Harries and Deborah Constant noted, 'Abortion access is … compromised by scarce facilities being concentrated mainly in urban centres, … [and] lack of information and support systems for women especially in poorer and hard to reach areas.'[7] Services in functioning facilities are fragmented according to the willingness of the health service providers to be involved in the various aspects of abortion care.[8] This results in facilities closing their abortion clinics if providers resign or move elsewhere. To exacerbate issues, facility, departmental and government officials often lack the political will to implement the CTOP Act.[9]

GESTATIONAL LIMITS: BEING TURNED AWAY AND LACK OF KNOWLEDGE

Termination of pregnancy is, obviously, a time-limited service. The CTOP Act differentiates between first- and second-trimester abortions. Second-trimester abortions are offered in fewer facilities than first-trimester abortions, which results in the need for referrals should a woman in her second trimester of pregnancy report to a facility only offering first-trimester procedures.

When participants in our study provided anecdotes of people they knew who wanted to but failed to abort, the reason always cited was that the public hospital turned the women away because their pregnancies were too far along. Whether these women were turned away from first- or second-trimester facilities is unclear. Failure to procure an abortion at a public hospital often leads desperate women to seek help from a traditional healer.

> An example is a person who went to have an abortion and was told that the pregnancy was far along. When you have reached a certain number of months, you cannot have an abortion. But she told herself that she is going to get an abortion. So a traditional man [corrects herself] woman arrived from the village and gave her something, and after that the abortion was completed in the house. But what happened then is the traditional healer ended up taking the woman's life, and she did not live. (Nasipi, rural town)

> If you are late and the baby has grown, then they are unable to assist you because the baby is too big. I have heard people going [away] from hospital since they were told they cannot be assisted when the baby is already grown. They go to these posters. I had a friend who passed away in 2015, who went to the hospital and was told that it's a full-grown baby and is moving, so they cannot

terminate. She went to the place which she saw in [nearby town]. She told me when she came back from this place that she saw a poster and went. After two days, I was here in [local town], and she was in [nearby town]. After two days, I got a call from her family saying that they found her dead in her room. She bled to death. So there is danger to it. (Bongiwe, rural town)

These tragic stories of unnecessary deaths from unsafe abortions performed by a traditional healer and an illegal provider reflect findings in research by Harries et al.[10] These researchers cited the following as some of the reasons for women accessing abortions late in their pregnancies: 'from inappropriate referrals and being sent from one facility to another before being seen, to waiting a further two weeks for an appointment as clinics were fully booked'.

While distance and costs may hamper women's ability to reach a facility in time, late presentation also has to do with women not knowing the legal stipulations around abortion or even that they are pregnant.

No, some don't end up getting abortions. They head that side, but then they are turned down, and they end up saying the girl is too far along in her pregnancy to terminate it. Because they're most likely just learning about the rules concerning abortion. They don't know the months and the rules. (Khunjulwa, remote village)

Some people cannot tell when they are pregnant. Maybe they only notice when they are two months and three weeks pregnant, and that's too far along in the pregnancy. (Esona, rural town)

Khunjulwa speaks to a lack of knowledge regarding the stipulations of the CTOP Act as a barrier. (Knowledge of abortion legislation is dealt with extensively in chapter 1.) The factor referred to by Esona – accurate pregnancy detection and correct gestation dating – has been highlighted in the literature. Moreover, deciding on an abortion requires knowledge of being pregnant. Some women consider waiting until the second or third month of a missed period before seeking pregnancy confirmation.[11] In rural areas, this may have to do with the costs of accessing a clinic or a pharmacy for pregnancy testing. In other words, some certainty (serial missed periods) is needed to justify the costs involved in confirming a pregnancy. The complication, however, is twofold: those wishing to take the pregnancy to term present late at antenatal clinics, a persistent problem in South Africa.[12] Those wishing to procure an abortion will have to fulfil the requirements for a second-trimester abortion and be able to travel to the few facilities that do offer them.

FEAR OF ABORTION OR THE CONSEQUENCES OF ABORTION

It was widely believed among our participants that abortion would lead to severe consequences.

> You get so heartbroken in such an unpleasant circumstance [unwanted pregnancy]. Others consider abortion but also reconsider that because of its associated risks, such as dying, and end up keeping the baby. (Esihle, remote village)
>
> You might die. If you are lucky enough and you do not die, you will not be well. Also, the child might be badly affected. (Funeka, remote village)
>
> Then to get out of such a situation, she will think the easiest way is to abort the pregnancy. However, some would keep the baby because of the fear of infertility in the future and end up [giving it up for] adoption and do other things. (Bamanye, rural town)
>
> I do not want to do that because sometimes, if I terminate a pregnancy, I might die or you find that my womb will never be okay. I will have issues with it my whole life. So it's better I keep the baby. (Khuselwa, commercial farming area)
>
> People are scared of dying, and now they don't want to do abortion but rather keep their children. (Aphelele, commercial farming area)

> There are [barriers] because maybe by getting an abortion, she will never have a child again. (Vuyo, commercial farming area)

In these extracts, the participants speak of abortion as leading to death, health problems and infertility. These perceived risks are depicted as being so entrenched that people will decide against abortion out of fear of such drastic consequences.

The irony in these statements is that implementation of the CTOP Act has resulted in decreased maternal morbidity and mortality.[13] Indeed, an abortion performed under safe conditions is safer than childbirth. In addition, as outlined in a review by Sam Rowlands:

> Women who have abortions are not at increased risk of mental health problems over and above women who deliver an unwanted pregnancy. There is no negative effect of abortion on a woman's subsequent fertility.[14]

Despite this, misinformation about abortion is widespread, dispersed partially by anti-abortion advocates. In our study, however, the fears referred to are in relation to unspecified abortion practices. It is entirely possible that the participants generalised the consequences of unsafe abortion to safe abortion services.

HEALTHCARE STAFF HOSTILITY TOWARDS ABORTION

Even though clinics and hospitals were seen as good sources of factual information, participants also spoke about poor treatment at healthcare facilities. Some of the descriptions did not have to do with abortion per se but with services in other areas.

> I do not know. They also discourage me at the hospitals. A person will go to the hospital to give birth, and they will just get shouted at at that hospital. (Bongani, remote village)

> You find that the pregnant woman, she does not want to go to
> the public clinic simply because she is not on good terms with cer-
> tain nurses who work there, and she will say she cannot go there
> because she assumes that the nurse with whom she has an issue
> will not treat her the same way as the other patients. She believes
> she will be mistreated because of the issue she has with the nurse.
> (Bulelani, rural town)

Bongani is referring to what is known as obstetric violence, which
includes, among other things, neglect, verbal and emotional abuse, physical abuse, sexual abuse, and lack of confidential and consensual care.
Its occurrence in public healthcare obstetric units in South Africa has
been documented.[15] Bulelani indicates that women will base their service
preferences on previous experiences at public clinics, where they may
have experienced discriminatory interactions.

Participants also spoke about healthcare workers not involved directly
in abortion care acting as barriers to services.

> They say you get there at the hospital and get told to decide if you
> want an abortion or what. When you get there, they do not treat
> you well when you are going to get an abortion. (Nasipi, rural town)
>
> So everyone who was there was alerted [that I requested an
> abortion], but since it was me, I didn't care. I waited for my folder.
> After she [the hospital clerk] was done cursing me, she gave me
> my folder. I left. Anyone could've been offended, but I didn't care
> because I already made a decision. (Bongiwe, rural town)

These participants relay how hospital administrators and front-line
health workers may ill-treat women who request an abortion. In relating
her personal story, Bongiwe depicts this behaviour as offensive and ver-
bally demonstrates her resistance to it (repeating that she 'didn't care').

Research elsewhere confirms that facility employees not directly
involved in abortion care may act as effective barriers to women accessing

the service.[16] This has consequences for women, some of whom have reported inappropriate referrals and being sent from one facility to another before being seen.[17] To reduce such dissuasion, value clarification and attitude transformation (VCAT) workshops were held by Ipas – an NGO seeking to improve access to safe abortion and contraception – with, among others, midwives and health facility managers.[18] Following the VCAT workshops, participants reported more behaviours supportive of the law and more compassion for women seeking abortions than before the workshops. However, these workshops have not been held regularly.

Participants also referred to abortion healthcare providers actively persuading women not to have an abortion.

> She [the nurse at the TOP clinic] will give you advice and even change your view. She could tell you to not terminate the pregnancy and might tell you how the child could come [in] handy in your old age. And you might begin to visualise your future. (Thato, rural town)
>
> Some people are afraid to go to the clinic because they get shouted at. People are sensitive. At the clinic they won't just take you to terminate, they will ask you questions. I think this is their way of determining if you are serious about what you want to do. (Esona, rural town)

Obtaining informed consent for an abortion requires that healthcare providers explain procedures. However, research conducted in South Africa has shown that nurses may try to dissuade particular people from having an abortion. This may involve creating a hierarchy of deserving clients, being dismissive of repeat abortions, suggesting that abortion leads to negative consequences, moralising about abortion, and pushing women to consider adoption, as found in research in the Eastern Cape by Jabulile Mavuso and Catriona Macleod.[19]

Negative healthcare provider attitudes are possibly related to conscientious objection – the opposition to the provision of a service healthcare workers morally disagree with. Conscientious objection regarding abortion has been debated rigorously in the international literature.[20] We do not repeat the complex arguments here except to indicate that some have renamed the action 'dishonourable disobedience'.[21] While the CTOP Act is silent about the right to conscientious objection, section 15 of the Constitution of South Africa implicitly accommodates conscientious objection to abortion.[22] Amnesty International identified the South African government's failure to regulate conscientious objection as a key impediment in accessing safe and legal abortion in the country.[23] Research by Harries et al. shows a general lack of understanding among health professionals concerning the circumstances in which they may invoke their right to refuse to provide or assist in abortion services.[24]

Our study indicated that judgemental healthcare provider attitudes did not apply to abortion alone but also to the assumption of carelessness in women with an unwanted pregnancy.

> Judgemental questions such as 'Why did you not protect yourself? Did you not know you could get pregnant?' discourage them so much that they end up taking the risk of seeking outside help, which is not safe. Or getting other pregnancy termination ideas from other people because they do not feel free to get safe abortions. (Ntobeko, rural town)

> At the hospital, she would receive information and details about contraceptive methods and where to access them. And the nurses will critically engage with the woman and ask her why she didn't make an effort not to get pregnant. Now she needs an abortion because she failed to do a, b and c. They will ask you the difficult questions, but ultimately, if you are certain about your decision to abort, then they won't stand in your way. (Bamanye, rural town)

Judgemental questions regarding contraceptive usage are depicted here as making people turn to informal or illegal abortion options.

PARTNER ATTITUDE

Partners can support abortion and provide the financial help a woman needs to have an abortion. Yet, partners can also be a significant barrier in a woman's decision making regarding abortion. Participants indicated that some women opt to abort without the partners' knowledge out of fear that their partner would terminate the relationship.

> You end up not being loved by the man whose baby you aborted. (Nasipi, rural town)
>
> She has had an abortion before, and after that her boyfriend stopped loving her due to her actions. (Azole, rural town)
>
> When I first met my boyfriend, I was 13 years old, and so I dated him and got pregnant when I was 15 years old ... He taught me how a man sleeps with a female, but after all that he turned against me. (Khuselwa, commercial farming area)

Participants speak here of a direct correlation between having an abortion and the conception partner no longer loving the woman or turning against her.

A major consideration was partners shaming the women in public for having undergone an abortion, even if they had agreed to terminating the pregnancy.

> For instance, if the guy that impregnated her knows that she terminated the baby, the guy will always say nasty things about her and call her all sorts of names because she aborted the baby. Therefore, she will be stigmatised for doing that, and the guy will be bitter about the fact that she aborted his child. So, every time the guy sees her with another man, he will always make funny comments so that she could feel guilty about the termination. As a result of that, it will be difficult for the girl to find another to be in love with. Therefore, she will have to go to another place in order

to be at peace and be away from the stigma that the guy has created for her … Even where the couple has agreed to get an abortion, and they will still continue dating, once they have an argument or a misunderstanding, the guy then will bring up the abortion thing as something to weaken her or make her feel guilty. (Bulelani, rural town)

He will ask her about it, and if it is true that she did abort, he might break up with her, and then he'll go around the community slandering and telling everyone what you did in order to humiliate you. (Gcobisa, remote village)

Given the high status in which fertility is held within the communities where we did our research, knowledge of an abortion can become a powerful weapon in a (former) partner's arsenal should he feel aggrieved with the woman or her decision to terminate the pregnancy. Participants refer here to men saying 'nasty things', calling women names and slandering them, resulting in guilt, weakness and humiliation. The fear of such things happening can be a powerful barrier to abortion access.

LACK OF INFORMATION AND KNOWLEDGE OF RIGHTS

Not knowing that abortion is a right or lacking basic information about the procedure was mentioned by participants as a barrier.

Although people do abortion, they hide it, and they do it while it is in the early stages. They are scared of it. They hide it. It's not out there yet. They do not know it is within their rights. (Siphamandla, rural town)

To be honest, a lot of people do not know. Many of the people who do know are those who have gone to work in places like big towns or cities, where they have heard that places to terminate pregnancies in a safe manner are available. There is no one at the local clinics or hospitals who has been given that information. The

> problem is that others do not have that information. (Ntobeko, rural town)
>
> Some still have the idea that you can be arrested for it. (Mpendulo, rural town)

Participants indicate that a lack of knowledge of the legality of abortion acts as a barrier to women accessing the service. Ntobeko refers to differences between urban and rural areas in terms of access to information. Knowledge of abortion legislation is dealt with in detail in chapter 1. What we highlight here is how lack of knowledge can lead to the same actions as abortion stigma does, as outlined by Siphamandla. In this case, however, concealment is resorted to because people misunderstand the legal situation regarding abortion and fear being accused of committing a crime.

CONCLUSION

In this chapter, we have described many structural and social issues that hinder women from accessing abortion. Structural barriers include the distance to facilities, the costs of procuring an abortion, the lack of functioning facilities, and the dearth of state-led information campaigns (leading to people lacking knowledge about their rights and about abortion services in general). Social barriers include breaches of confidentiality by facility staff, inaccurate information about the health consequences of safe abortion, partner attitudes and stigmatisation, and healthcare staff hostility towards abortion. Of course, structural and social barriers overlap. For example, if a healthcare facility manager is hostile towards abortion, it is likely that the resources to maintain and staff an abortion clinic will not be made available.

The barriers noted in this chapter may lead women to seek abortions outside of the formal sector or to present for an abortion in the second trimester. Women may turn to illegal providers who advertise via posters in urban centres, traditional healers or self-induction. It is estimated that about half of abortions are performed outside the formal sector and that about a quarter of abortions performed in the formal sector are conducted in the second trimester.[25] While some of the barriers discussed here apply across urban and rural locations, such as the lack of state-led information campaigns, others, such as distances to facilities, apply specifically in rural areas. With this in mind, it is crucial to ascertain rural people's preferences for abortion services. These are explored in the next chapter.

6

The Conundrum of Confidentiality Versus Cost: Abortion Service Provision Preferences

In this chapter we outline the results of the discrete choice experiment (DCE) we conducted in the three rural areas that formed part of this study. As indicated in the introduction, DCEs allow researchers to investigate how people in a particular context rate selected attributes of a service by asking them to state their preference for different hypothetical alternatives. Using a DCE, we can identify what factors play a role when people choose an abortion provider. The data from our DCE provide a range of information, such as the ideal location or opening hours of abortion clinics or how much people are willing to pay to have an abortion. This type of information can be used by an array of people and institutions, both public and private, in planning and providing abortion services that are suitable to the context, which in this case is rural South Africa.

An initial analysis of the qualitative data generated in the study focused on identifying attributes of abortion care to inform the quantitative component of the research. This analysis, along with input from the expert panel, was used in the construction of the DCE questionnaire. The following attributes were identified: facility type, services offered, abortion type, location of the facility, cost and facility opening hours. In addition to demographic questions related to age, sex and employment status, we asked the following ranking questions in the DCE questionnaire: 'What would be the most important to you, or someone like you, in choosing a provider? Please rate your choice: 1 being your top choice and 4 being your last choice' (choices were the type of facility, location, cost, opening hours)'; and 'If you, or someone like you, wished to have an abortion, which provider would you/they choose? Please rate your choice: 1 being your top choice and 5 being your last choice' (choices were government service, informal provider, traditional healer, self-abortion and private provider). The DCE questionnaire was translated into isiXhosa and then back-translated to ensure conceptual and linguistic equivalence (see figure 0.1 in the introduction for an example of one of the ten choice tasks in the DCE questionnaire).

Multinomial logistic regressions (MLRs) were run for the pooled sample and by sex and site to explore preference differences among these groups. It should be noted, however, that preferences among women, rather than men, more strongly influenced results from the pooled sample, as the sample size of women was much larger than that of men.

RANKED FACTORS IN CHOOSING A FACILITY OR PROVIDER

Respondents were asked which of the following factors would be the most important in choosing a provider: type of facility, location, cost and opening hours. Respondents could specify a first and a second preference. Overall, the type of facility ranked as the most important factor and opening hours the least important. However, the differences between the factors are minor, suggesting that all the factors play some role.

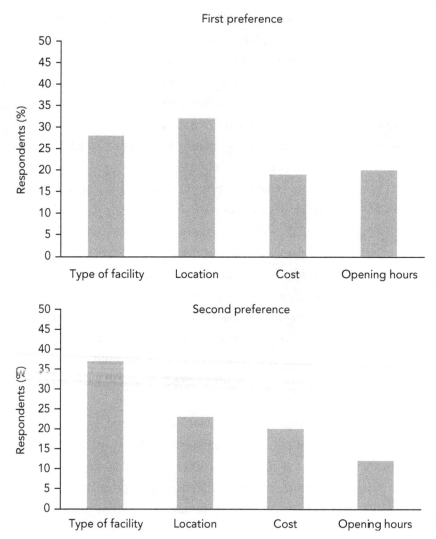

Figure 6.1: First and second preferences of factors in choosing an abortion services provider

Figure 6.1 charts the number of respondents indicating a first and second preference regarding the above-mentioned factors. While type of facility is ranked lower than location as the first preference, it tops the second-preference list. Overall, therefore, type of facility emerged as the most important factor, but not by much.

As indicated at the start of this book, we undertook this research to inform Marie Stopes South Africa about these communities' preferences regarding abortion services, as Marie Stopes wished to extend their services to rural areas. Part of this process was to ascertain whether private abortion services would indeed be used and welcomed. Respondents were thus asked which type of service they, or somebody like them, would choose if they needed to have an abortion: government service, traditional healer, self-abortion, private provider or informal provider. Fieldworkers explained to respondents what a Marie Stopes clinic is and what accessing an abortion there would entail (a safe but not free service). Again, respondents could specify a first and second preference. Overall, government services were the most chosen, followed by traditional healers. Informal providers were the least preferred. Private providers ranked just above informal providers, possibly because of cost and possibly owing to a lack of familiarity with such providers in rural areas. Figure 6.2 shows the first and second preferences for type of abortion services provider.

The preference for government clinics was also evident in the qualitative data. Despite concerns about breaches of confidentiality and some complaints about the quality of care provided at public facilities, participants said they would suggest going to government clinics or hospitals for abortion information or abortion care. The use of public clinics was justified as being the safest option.

> I think the main reasons to go to hospital is safety and it's legal, so [it's] the simplest way that you do the right thing, you know you won't be harmed, there are no complications. You will be treated well, rather than hearing [ordinary] people tell you what to do or what to take. The only right way is the hospital. (Andisiwe, rural town)
>
> I chose the hospital because I felt safe. There was an experienced doctor, and I didn't care what people said about me. But no one is judged at the hospital. They respect your decision. (Bongiwe, rural town)

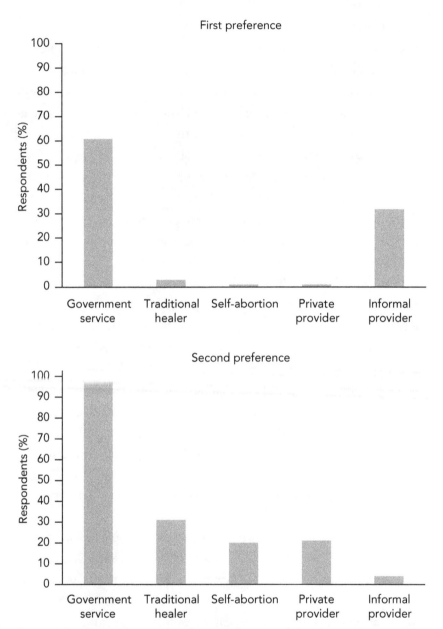

Figure 6.2: First and second preferences for type of abortion services provider

When you do not go to the right places, the hospital, and you listen to other people's ideas, you can be in danger of dying, you and the baby that you were aborting. You did not go to a place that offers the right help. That is why you should go to the right places, like the hospital, to go get the right clarification so that you do not take other substances. (Siphamandla, rural town)

Here the spectre of unsafe abortion looms large. Government hospitals are viewed as the safest option. Given the resource-poor nature of these communities, private service providers are often not available or financially accessible and so they are not used as a comparison in these narratives. However, one participant said they would choose a private clinic to avoid a breach of confidentiality at a public facility.

The question of safety was a prominent topic of conversation. It was well known among the participants that illegal providers ('those with the posters'), traditional healers and home-made concoctions are unsafe. No participant in the qualitative component suggested that abortion seekers should use these providers/methods, although they had opinions on why they might want to.

> An example would be me paying R300 to someone who is going to get plants and herbs that they will know will work. I don't have to travel; this person stays here in the village. I'll drink the mixture and be fine, but I won't really be fine because it is not the same as going to the hospital. The problem is that I do not have the money. (Fezeka, remote village)
>
> I would say if they do not have any other way, they must do it the traditional way, like how I have explained that people do it by combining different things. Because in this case, they do not want people to know, and going to the hospital will be a problem. (Esona, rural town)

Here confidentiality and cost are provided as reasons why people may seek illegal or traditional providers. However, participants stressed that this option should be a last resort ('I won't really be fine'; 'if they do not have any other way').

Tables 6.1 and 6.2 present data on preferences for the services offered at a clinic. These tables show preferences for extended services – abortion and contraceptive services, and abortion with other health services – in relation to abortion-only services. In other words, abortion-only services are the base against which preferences for extended services are measured. In table 6.1, the pooled data and data from women respondents show a very strong preference for abortion to be offered with other health services (statistically significant at the $p < 0.01$ level means that there is less than a 1% chance that the preferences measured are random). While abortion offered with contraceptive services is preferred over abortion services only, combining abortion with other health services is the most preferred option. This result is consistent across all three sites, as noted in table 6.2, indicating a robust finding regarding service offerings in rural areas of the Eastern Cape. Male respondents, once again, were more neutral in their selections, with no specific preference for services emerging as statistically significant over others.

Table 6.1: MLR coefficients for services offered (pooled sample and by sex)

Services offered (vs abortion only)	Pooled	Female	Male
Abortion and other health services	0.658*** (0.138)	0.824*** (0.153)	−0.009 (0.328)
Abortion and contraceptives	0.332*** (0.076)	0.375*** (0.084)	0.086 (0.180)

***$p < 0.01$

Note: Standard errors in parentheses.

Table 6.2: MLR coefficients for services offered by site

Services offered (vs abortion only)	Remote village	Rural town	Commercial farming area
Abortion and other health services	0.612** (0.253)	0.773*** (0.248)	0.836*** (0.239)
Abortion and contraceptives	0.099 (0.134)	0.544*** (0.144)	0.527*** (0.130)

**$p < 0.05$; ***$p < 0.01$

Note: Standard errors in parentheses.

The qualitative data also revealed a dislike for stand-alone abortion clinics. Those participants who had an opinion on what a clinic that offers abortions should look like suggested that it should not actively present itself as an abortion clinic.

> Firstly, it is because the people of this village are very judgemental, and it affects people so badly they end up not being okay. So, if it is labelled 'counselling', whoever goes to the clinic will assume that the person who goes into that room has had an abortion, or that is why they are coming out of there. That rumour will go around the village, and people will talk about you based on that assumption. As you walk out of there, you will even notice people standing there and staring at you with judgement. (Ntobeko, rural town)
>
> In my opinion, they would see it as any other clinic that helps people because it would not be restricted to services for women. It would have general services. If a clinic would have services for everyone, it would not be seen as a clinic, that is – how do you say in Xhosa? – as one that is befouled [sinister], that kills people's children. But it should be a clinic with all services, you see? (Nandi, commercial farming area)

Here participants emphasise once again the imperative of confidentiality. Ntobeko indicates that even a place offering abortion counselling should consider mystifying its official purpose. Some participants indicated that people might believe that a stand-alone abortion clinic is actively persuading women to have abortions.

PREFERENCES IN THE LOCATION OF ABORTION FACILITIES

In table 6.3, preferences are outlined for the location of facilities outside the respondents' village – in the nearest city, a nearby village or the nearest town. Negative scores indicate a lower preference for the location in relation to own village. Pooled quantitative data revealed a strong preference

Table 6.3:   MLR coefficients for facility location (pooled sample and by sex)

Location of facility (vs in my village)	Pooled	Female	Male
Nearest city	−0.037 (0.088)	0.023 (0.098)	−0.221 (0.210)
Nearby village	−0.359*** (0.070)	−0.519*** (0.079)	0.267* (0.162)
Nearest town	−0.413*** (0.091)	−0.571*** (0.101)	0.211 (0.220)

*p < 0.1; ***p < 0.01

Note: Standard errors in parentheses.

for facilities within the respondents' village rather than in a nearby village or the nearest town. Preference for facilities in the nearest city was slightly weaker than the preference for a facility in the respondents' village, but this was not statistically significant. This finding may be related to the central conundrum captured in this study: confidentiality versus cost. The strong preference for facilities to be located in the respondents' village relates to the concern about cost (financial and opportunity). The slightly weaker preference for a facility in the nearest city speaks to the question of anonymity and the reduced risk of breaches of confidentiality. Overall, male respondents had less firm preferences than women.

Disaggregation by site reveals a slightly different picture, as seen in table 6.4. The remote village and the commercial farming area follow the pattern of the pooled data, with preferences for facilities in their village or in the nearest city (the commercial farming area has a slight preference for location in the nearest city over the respondents' village). The rural town's results show no statistical differences between the various options, with a slight preference for location in the nearest town.

Interpreting these differences in results is complicated. In expressing a preference regarding the location of facilities, as indicated above, respondents are likely weighing up confidentiality against distance and cost. The fact that the data from the rural town differ from that of the other two sites in the expression of location preference may have to do with the rural town's relative proximity to a small town and a major city. Respondents may not feel that going to the nearest city is any different

Table 6.4:   MLR coefficients for facility location by site

Location of facility (vs in my village)	Remote village	Rural town	Commercial farming area
Nearest city	−0.060 (0.155)	−0.046 (0.161)	0.131 (0.153)
Nearby village	−0.529*** (0.126)	−0.095 (0.130)	−0.438*** (0.118)
Nearest town	−0.980*** (0.163)	0.014 (0.171)	−0.472*** (0.159)

***p < 0.01

Note: Standard errors in parentheses.

from going to the nearest town. In this site, location in a nearby village is the least preferred (although this is not statistically significant in relation to the clinic location being in their own village).

In the qualitative component, participants indicated that if a local institution could ensure confidentiality, people would use it.

> If there was a clinic, they would go to the clinic … If you felt safe with the fact that they will not disclose your problem to other people so that you will not be humiliated, [you would go there]. (Gcobisa, remote village)
>
> It's important [that the abortion facility] be a safe place. I must not be sitting and waiting to abort in an open room. It must be a safe place, and a trustworthy person must do this. It can't be a place where suddenly the door is opened, and passers-by are looking in the window to see what I was doing. (Andisiwe, rural town)

Confidentiality – the concern that nurses not divulge the participant's situation and the desire for absolute privacy – was emphasised as necessary. Only under these circumstances would people feel safe and hence use the facility.

PREFERENCES IN FACILITY OPENING TIMES

Tables 6.5 and 6.6 contain analyses of responses to facility opening times in relation to 8:30–16:30 Monday to Friday. The options for opening

Table 6.5: MLR coefficients for facility opening times (pooled sample and by sex)

Opening times (vs 8:30–16:30 Monday to Friday)	Pooled	Female	Male
8:30–22:00 Monday to Friday	0.198*** (0.040)	0.266*** (0.044)	−0.074 (0.095)
8:30–16:30 Monday to Saturday	0.171*** (0.059)	0.227*** (0.066)	0.009 (0.140)
8:30–22:00 Monday to Saturday	−0.106* (0.061)	−0.073 (0.068)	−0.199 (0.150)

*p < 0.1; ***p < 0.01

Note: Standard errors in parentheses.

times included extended hours within the working week; regular office hours but with the addition of Saturday; and a combination of the above. Pooled data revealed a strong preference for extended hours during the week, followed by a more or less equally strong preference for regular office hours, Monday to Saturday. Interestingly, the combination of both (Saturday and extended hours) was not favoured. This may have to do with respondents' appreciation of the logistical difficulties in keeping facilities open for such a long time and an awareness that such an arrangement is unlikely. Although men and women differed slightly in their preferences, it is clear that both prefer facilities to operate outside of weekly office hours, whether through extension into the evening or to Saturday.

When the data are disaggregated across sites, differences in preferences for operating hours emerge, as seen in table 6.6. Extending hours to Saturday is the strongly preferred option for respondents from the remote village. This may have to do with the relative distance of this site from towns or cities. People may be unable to take advantage of evening opening times because of the distance they have to travel home from the facility. Respondents in the commercial farming area indicated a more or less equal preference for extended evening hours and the extension to Saturday. Rural town respondents strongly preferred extended evening hours, followed by a preference for facilities to be open on Saturdays.

Table 6.6: MLR coefficients for facility opening times by site

Opening times (vs 8:30–16:30 Monday to Friday)	Remote village	Rural town	Commercial farming area
8:30–22:00 Monday to Friday	0.022 (0.071)	0.218*** (0.069)	0.323*** (0.073)
8:30–16:30 Monday to Saturday	0.305*** (0.105)	−0.204* (0.109)	0.385*** (0.102)
8:30–22:00 Monday to Saturday	−0.028 (0.108)	−0.417*** (0.117)	−0.016 (0.105)

*p < 0.1; ***p < 0.01

Note: Standard errors in parentheses.

The preferences expressed in the rural town and the commercial farming area may have to do with these sites' relative proximity to towns where facilities may be located. Regarding this preference, it may be best to extend hours to Saturdays to cover far-flung rural areas and those closer to facilities.

RANKED PREFERENCES IN INFORMATION CHANNELS

Respondents were asked to rank the information channels from which they would like to receive information about abortion. The results are given in table 6.7. Pamphlets or posters were ranked the highest among the information channels, and the internet (online) was ranked the lowest. Grouping the sources together, it appears that non-interactive media (pamphlets, posters, radio and TV) are the most popular sources (see figure 6.3). This is followed by trusted others, including family, friends and home-based carers. Formal sources of information, including teachers and nurses, are ranked lower than these trusted others. Toll-free numbers and online sources are the least popular, possibly because of a lack of familiarity with working through the menus that come with phoning toll-free numbers or the poor access to Wi-Fi in rural communities.

Table 6.7:   Ranking of information sources about abortion

	Mean rank*	Marginal frequency**	
		1st preference	2nd preference
Information channel			
Pamphlets/posters	3.93	175	51
Radio/TV	4	130	79
Friends/family	4.34	78	65
Home-based carer	4.43	29	59
School/university	4.37	94	67
Nurse	4.44	68	60
Toll-free number	4.67	21	48
Online	4.77	17	40

Mean rank tells how popular a certain option is. Note that a higher rank means a lower number, as 1 is the highest rank

**Marginal frequencies describe how many times an option is put at this ranking spot.*

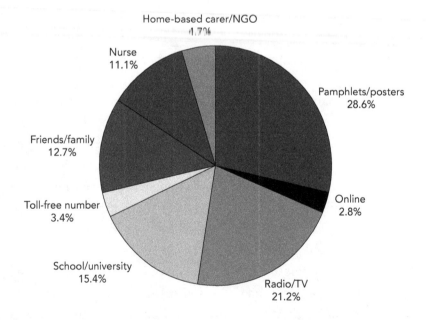

Figure 6.3:   First preference for source of abortion information

CONCLUSION

In this chapter, we outline the results of the DCE we conducted in the three rural areas that formed part of this study. The quantitative data revealed that all the factors asked about concerning abortion services affect respondents' preferences – facility type, services offered, abortion type, location, cost and opening hours. Results concerning preferences in facility type suggest that abortions provided in public hospitals and medical abortions, at least provided in mobile clinics, are the most preferred and viable service options. The ideal facility type would depend on the context of the rural site. Stand-alone clinics are not recommended. The most robust finding across all sites was the strong preference for abortion to be offered alongside other health services. This finding dovetails with the qualitative findings regarding confidentiality. Locating clinics within government facilities or a pharmacy would assist with this. If mobile clinics are used as well, or if clinics are located within villages, then offering non-reproductive health services alongside sexual and reproductive services should be considered.

Respondents preferred services located in their village or the nearest city. These preferences probably relate to the balance of cost, distance and confidentiality. The varying results across sites suggest that a catchment area approach to the location of facilities may work best. Those rural areas close to towns or cities may be serviced by facilities in towns or cities, while those further afield may also need services within their own village, probably in the form of mobile clinics or clinics that partner with local NGOs. Respondents strongly preferred extended operating hours, although preferences for when hours should be extended differed across sites. Respondents across all sites recognised the difficulties of providing extended evening and weekend hours. The latter is recommended in the trade-off of providing extended evening hours during the week or extended hours over weekends. This would ensure that women in far-flung rural areas as well as those close to towns and cities may access services outside of regular weekday operating hours. Alternatively, if a dual catchment area approach is taken, as suggested above, hours could be adjusted to suit the type of clinic. Clinics in towns or cities could operate with extended evening hours, while clinics in villages (mobile or in conjunction with local NGOs) could operate on Saturdays. Rural villages mostly lack street lighting, so extended evening hours are not feasible within these locations.

In the concluding chapter, we reflect on the findings of our study using the reparative justice approach and make recommendations regarding how safe, comprehensive abortion care could be improved in rural areas.

A s indicated in the introduction to this book, the CTOP Act states that 'the State has the responsibility to provide reproductive health *to all*, and also to provide *safe conditions* under which the right of choice can be exercised'.[1] Our study's findings clearly illustrate that in terms of abortion services in rural areas, the provision of care 'to all' has not been fulfilled. In support of this assertion are the stories participants in our study told of women dying from accessing illegal providers. The provision of 'safe conditions' has also not been realised. Our participants spoke repeatedly and in depth about fears of breaches of confidentiality, debilitating stigma and many structural barriers to accessing abortion services.

In their systematic review of abortion care indicators, Amanda Dennis et al. signal little agreement in the literature on the indicators of quality abortion care. While certain indicators (e.g., good infrastructure and training) may be accepted as applying across contexts, there is also a strong need to hone services to particular contexts.[2]

In this concluding chapter, we highlight the significance and implications of our findings for the future of abortion services in rural areas in South Africa. To foreground the cross-cutting and contextual issues that need addressing, we adopt a reparative justice approach as outlined and developed by Catriona Macleod and colleagues.[3]

REPARATIVE REPRODUCTIVE JUSTICE

The reproductive justice approach interweaves rights-based understandings of reproduction and social justice principles.[4] A range of

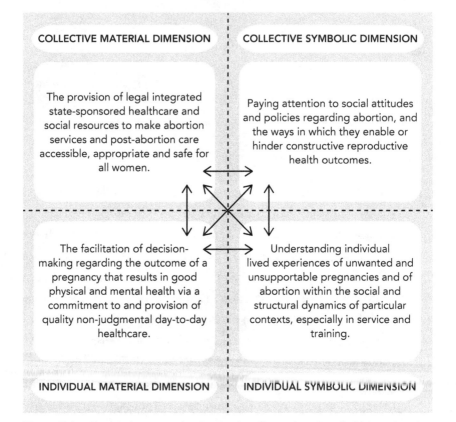

COLLECTIVE MATERIAL DIMENSION

The provision of legal integrated state-sponsored healthcare and social resources to make abortion services and post-abortion care accessible, appropriate and safe for all women.

COLLECTIVE SYMBOLIC DIMENSION

Paying attention to social attitudes and policies regarding abortion, and the ways in which they enable or hinder constructive reproductive health outcomes.

The facilitation of decision-making regarding the outcome of a pregnancy that results in good physical and mental health via a commitment to and provision of quality non-judgmental day-to-day healthcare.

Understanding individual lived experiences of unwanted and unsupportable pregnancies and of abortion within the social and structural dynamics of particular contexts, especially in service and training.

INDIVIDUAL MATERIAL DIMENSION

INDIVIDUAL SYMBOLIC DIMENSION

Figure 7.1: Reparative reproductive justice dimensions in relation to abortion care

critical theoretical approaches underpins social justice thinking and practice. Common to them all is an understanding that 'society is stratified (divided and unequal) in significant and far-reaching ways along social group lines that include race, class, gender, sexuality and ability'.[5] Overcoming inequities in various domains is a key focus of the approach.

Reproductive justice implies an analysis that brings the intertwining of individual and social processes to the fore. The ultimate aim is to ensure the rights of people to (1) have children; (2) not have children; and (3) raise children in supportive, safe and healthy environments, all within conditions of their choosing. In general, reparative justice implies recompense or restitution for an injustice in which a person's rights and/ or interests have been harmed.

Drawing on the interweaving of the politics of distribution and of recognition – and in support of recommendations for action – the reparative justice model, as outlined by Ernesto Verdeja and extended by Macleod and colleagues, involves analyses of two sets of conditions: material/ objective conditions and symbolic/subjective, identity-based conditions.[6] These are analysed at two levels: individual and collective. The combination of conditions and levels allows for four 'ideal-typical' dimensions to be analysed: individual material; collective material; individual symbolic; and collective symbolic. The implications of these dimensions concerning abortion care are outlined in figure 7.1.

In the following, we summarise the findings of our study under each of the reparative justice dimensions. We highlight the injustices evident in our data and bring them together in summary form with recommendations for overcoming them.

COLLECTIVE MATERIAL DIMENSION

> *The provision of legal integrated state-sponsored healthcare and social resources to make abortion services and post-abortion care accessible, appropriate and safe for all women.*

Knowledge dissemination

While participants in the study seemed to have reasonable knowledge that abortion is legal (with some notable exceptions), their understandings of the stipulations of the CTOP Act, the location of abortion clinics and abortion procedures were sketchy. Some blatantly false or catastrophising narratives were presented, especially concerning the potential consequences of abortion. This may result from participants having experience with illegal or unsafe abortions rather than abortions performed in designated government or private clinics. Participants knew about traditional healers as potential providers but did not trust them in this capacity. Local abortifacients and various concoctions to induce abortion were also mentioned. Stories about women losing their lives due to unsafe abortion speak to the lack of knowledge of post-abortion care, among other things.

The most trusted source of information for an individual seeking information about accessing an abortion was public clinics. Regarding general information about abortion, the quantitative data showed that respondents prefer traditional non-interactive media (pamphlets, posters, radio and TV) followed by trusted others, including family, friends and home-based carers.

It is clear that much work is needed to ensure widespread knowledge about (1) the legality of abortion; (2) the stipulations of the CTOP Act; (3) the minimal risks of safe abortion (compared to taking unwanted pregnancy to term); (4) the location of clinics; (5) the risks of unsafe abortion and the need to avoid illegal providers; and (6) where and how to access post-abortion care. The medium of communication is also important. Countering the ubiquitous posters advertising illegal abortion services requires equal verve alongside distributing pamphlets and posters with factual information on legal services, particularly through public health clinics (which were seen by our participants as trustworthy places to access information). Given the remoteness of many rural areas, using local and community radio stations for public information campaigns would be particularly beneficial. As outlined by Frans Krüger, there is 'a plethora of community stations across the country ... [and] in some very remote areas'.[7] Home-based carers or community health workers could assist in the informal dissemination of knowledge through their care networks. If home-based carers provide detailed and accurate information to community members during their visits, better information may be passed on between friends and family members, the second most-preferred source of information. Partnering with NGOs or local community groups, especially women's groups or church groups (if they are not anti-abortion), could assist in this regard.

Integrative services

The integration of safe, legal abortion within broader sexual and reproductive health services, including in relation to HIV care, is essential. This is particularly important as research shows that stigma and misinformation around HIV and HIV care may form a part of women's decision making on abortion and of healthcare providers' interactions with HIV-positive women seeking an abortion.[8] Research by Phyllis Orner et al. shows that HIV-positive women often fear that pregnancy can worsen their health, a concern that intersects with the fear that a pregnancy can cause additional socio-economic hardship. Orner et al. recommend creating stronger linkages between HIV care and abortion care services.[9]

Providing contraception, testing for sexually transmitted infections (STIs), pregnancy tests, antenatal care and other gynaecological services would render the clinic an asset to the community. Providing integrative services is less likely to draw conservative community members' ire when they find out that abortions are performed at the clinic. Women going there would simply be seen as going for any one of the services.

Although traditional healers as abortion providers were viewed with suspicion, many still operate in rural areas and are often the first port of call for health-related matters. Discussions between the Department of Health and traditional healers about referrals for safe abortion and post-abortion care could prove helpful. It is also important to recognise that South Africa has various categories of traditional healers and their practices are not well regulated. It is possible that experiences with abortifacients relayed by our study participants were provided by untrained and unregistered local healers or fake traditional healers, of which there are many.[10]

Setting up clinics near or next to NGO facilities could help integrate new clinics into the community, and NGO home-based carers, where they exist, can draw from the clinic's knowledge and services. NGOs should provide their home-based carers with accurate knowledge concerning women's rights under the CTOP Act and the abortion procedure itself, along with training in the importance of confidentiality. Although many NGO health workers are not in favour of abortion, training could increase their understanding of the importance of the procedure in reproductive health. All the home-based carers with whom we worked during this study were willing to participate, and many of them gave thanks for receiving information on the topic since they could now provide it to the people with whom they worked in the community.

Respondents indicated a preference for services located in their village or nearest city. These preferences probably relate to balancing cost, distance and confidentiality. The varying results across sites suggest that a dual catchment area approach to the location of facilities may work best. Facilities in towns or cities may service those rural areas close to them. Those living further afield may also need services within their village, probably in the form of mobile clinics or clinics that partner with local NGOs.

COLLECTIVE SYMBOLIC DIMENSION

> *Paying attention to social attitudes and policies regarding abortion, and the ways in which they enable or hinder constructive reproductive health outcomes.*

Staff approaches and support

A robust finding of this study was the oft-repeated fear of breaches of confidentiality and the possibility of encountering judgemental attitudes among healthcare providers. This extends to referring staff as well as abortion providers.

All employees working at clinics or in outreach services need to understand the importance of not breaching confidentiality. Where healthcare providers are drawn from the local community, additional emphasis should be placed on confidentiality, stressing the adverse outcomes of breaches of privacy. In-depth discussions around reproductive health issues in general, and abortion specifically, would be needed.

Research conducted in the Eastern Cape has found that abortion counselling is often directive and harmful to women.[11] Such directiveness, the researchers argue, draws on anti-abortion rhetoric and aims to dissuade women from having an abortion. In line with the clearly stated need for non-judgemental healthcare, abortion care providers should be trained in person-centred and non-directive abortion counselling. The guidelines developed by Jabulile Mavuso et al., based on data collected in the Eastern Cape, could prove useful in training counsellors.[12]

It is important to realise that while women who choose to have an abortion experience significant stigma, health professionals who offer the service may also face negativity. South African research indicates that stigma toward abortion health service providers manifests as name-calling, harassment and intimidation.[13] Institutional- and peer-support mechanisms (e.g., regular debriefing sessions that bring providers together) and a positive work environment could assist in managing stigma.

Community attitudes and stigma

In the rural areas where we did our research, we found general negativity towards abortion. Abortion was opposed on moral as well as health grounds: as an act of murder or sin as well as leading to psychological or physical fallout, in particular infertility. Provisional acceptance (particularly in the case of rape) and some differences of opinion were reported by participants, but the general feeling was that abortion should be avoided.

These negative attitudes towards abortion were evident in various forms of overt discrimination referred to by participants. Verbal abuse and gossip were said to be the most common forms of being singled out. Being judged, laughed at, called a murderer, humiliated, scolded and constantly reminded in a condemnatory way that one had had an abortion were often mentioned by participants. Some participants mentioned the likelihood of having the police called on them or of being chased out of the community. There were also mentions of women leaving the area after negative judgement and gossip became too much to handle.

According to our participants, managing the stigma attached to abortion required concealment. This would be enacted through seeking abortion services outside the area, keeping the abortion a secret and going to trusted service providers (i.e., those known to maintain confidentiality – often illegal providers, even if they are known to be unsafe). This behaviour is known in the literature as maintaining a good reputation. Managing a damaged reputation, where the abortion has become known, requires normalising the abortion experience. This did not appear much in the data, although there were glimmers thereof.

Anuradha Kumar et al. argue that abortion stigma is a 'compound stigma': 'it builds on other forms of discrimination and structural injustices'.[14] In our data, participants spoke to several stigmatic events, including refusal to fulfil compulsory motherhood (for women of a certain age), pregnancy among teenage women, HIV stigma, and sex outside of wedlock or multiple partners.

Researchers who study abortion stigma suggest a variety of possible forms of intervention. Some interventions are focused on building the resilience of the stigmatised.[15] (This is taken up further in the individual symbolic dimension section of this chapter.) Other approaches focus on reforming the language used in medical schools regarding abortion.[16] Still others target community beliefs and attitudes and work on fostering empathy.[17] All of these interventions are important in a multifaceted approach to reducing abortion stigma.

Large organisations have also produced a variety of toolkits for those who want to launch an intervention against abortion stigma.[18] For example, the Ipas manual 'Abortion Stigma Ends Here' is designed for staff or members of community-based organisations and NGOs, community health workers and community members.[19] The manual provides a number of interactive activities to decrease stigma at the community level and can be adapted for use depending on context.

Some research has shown that these community-level kinds of interactions can reduce stigma. Fiona Bloomer et al., for example, evaluated whether informal adult education in women's centres could foster resistance to the otherwise highly patriarchal anti-abortion stance in Northern Ireland. These settings, they found, created dialogical spaces that could lead to a reduction of stigmatising attitudes.[20]

Another increasingly popular community-level intervention is online storytelling. This involves publishing individual abortion stories online (by organisations such as Abortion Out Loud, 2+ Abortions, Voices of Courage, We Testify, The Abortion Diary, and Shout Your Abortion). Online campaigns have been met with ambivalence, however. While many have praised the women for their bravery in sharing their stories, this tactic has not had success in changing the minds of those who are already anti-abortion.[21] Moreover, some of these campaigns have been met with dedicated counter-attacks. Emboldened anti-abortion groups have used these online storytelling campaigns to stoke anti-abortion sentiments. In addition, given that people living in resource-poor rural areas have limited access to digital technologies, this kind of intervention is unlikely to have the desired effect in these areas.

A key problem for abortion stigma reduction programmes is that deep-rooted inequalities impact women's reproductive choices.[22] As noted by our participants, unmarried women, young women, women living with HIV and poor women are likely to attract negative attention from communities for various reproductive health activities (e.g., teenagers seeking contraception or pregnancy tests). Participants did speak about personal circumstances despite not being asked to tell personal stories or anecdotes about other community members. In narrating these stories, participants provided rich contextual information promoting empathy for the women's actions. Incorporating these broader reproductive stories with relevant contextual information can be a powerful tool to deflect stigma, promote understanding and normalise abortion as a standard reproductive health service. The sources of knowledge dissemination referred to earlier in this chapter could also be used for such storytelling.

The inequities around reproductive health issues are linked to the strong preference among our participants for abortion to be offered alongside other health services. This is where the collective material dimension of reparative justice interweaves with the collective symbolic dimension. Offering some non-reproductive health services alongside sexual and reproductive services – e.g., vaccinations and basic screenings – could help obviate the stigma that may accrue to particular women who access a range of reproductive health services.

INDIVIDUAL MATERIAL DIMENSION

> *The facilitation of decision making regarding the outcome of a pregnancy that results in good physical and mental health via a commitment to and provision of quality non-judgemental day-to-day healthcare.*

We conducted our research in resource-poor rural areas. The fact that participants frequently mentioned poverty as a factor in the decision-making process regarding the outcome of a pregnancy is not surprising. In addition, some participants mentioned the lack of quality antenatal care in the area as a possible reason for abortion. These factors point to the material conditions that constrain women's reproductive decision making.

Distance and costs

A reality in rural areas is that clinics are often inaccessible. Accessing an abortion frequently means significant financial expenditure, not just on the procedure itself, but also on travelling, accommodation, pain medication, sanitary pads and opportunity costs. The length of queues at facilities, the possibility of not having a same-day procedure, being turned away from overfull clinics and the need to travel even further for second-trimester abortions contribute significantly towards abortion-related costs. Opportunity costs could include income loss from informal work or missed classes.

Where rural villages are spread over hundreds of square kilometres, these challenges will be difficult to overcome and will likely require a range of approaches to cope with them. These could include:

1. increasing the number of clinics, including mobile clinics, that offer abortion services in rural towns using a catchment approach;
2. limiting the number of visits that rural women have to make to the clinics;
3. telephonic consultations;
4. extending hours of operation of clinics; and
5. improving early pregnancy detection.

Regarding the first recommendation, the results of our DCE point to the possibility of a dual catchment area approach to providing services in rural areas. Those living in rural areas close to towns or cities may be serviced by facilities in towns or cities, while those who live further afield may also need services within their own village, probably in the form of mobile clinics. Importantly, no clinic should be identifiable as offering abortion services only. Instead, abortion should be provided as part of other healthcare services.

The second recommendation points to the need for same-day services, especially in the first trimester. As most women have decided the outcome of the pregnancy before accessing services, it is vital that, whenever possible, (non-mandatory) counselling, consent and the procedure are scheduled for the same day. Follow-up can occur telephonically where possible. This relates to the third recommendation.

The third recommendation has recently received significant attention in the abortion services literature. Self-managed abortion via telemedicine involves a telephonic or video consultation between a healthcare provider and a client, wherein the client is guided through the process of taking the medical abortion pills that had been posted to them. A systematic review of medical abortion telemedicine found that 'medical abortion through telemedicine seems to be highly acceptable to women and providers, [and] success rate and safety outcomes are similar to those reported in literature for in-person abortion care'.[23] Given the reasonably high penetration of cellphones in South Africa, medical abortion telemedicine may be possible. It is estimated that 87% of the country's population own a phone, 8% do not own a phone but share one and 5% have no access at all to a phone.[24] Network access is not even, of course, and rural areas experience lower levels of access than urban areas. Data costs are also high in South Africa. While telemedicine could assist with the negative factors of distance and costs involved in abortion care, caution would have to be exercised in cases where women share a phone with others: such sharing could compromise confidentiality.

Participants strongly preferred extended operating hours, although the preferences for when hours should be extended differed across sites. Participants across all sites recognised the difficulties of providing extended evening and weekend hours. The latter is recommended in the trade-off of providing extended evening hours during the week or extended hours over weekends. This will ensure that women in far-flung rural areas and those near facilities may access services outside of standard weekday operating hours. Alternatively, if a dual catchment area approach is taken, as suggested above, hours could be adjusted to suit the type of clinic. Clinics in towns or cities could operate with extended evening hours, while clinics in villages (mobile or in conjunction with local NGOs) could operate on Saturdays. Given that rural villages mostly lack street lighting and public transport, extended evening hours are not feasible within these locations.[25]

Travel distance and costs are increased for women presenting for second-trimester abortions. These procedures are more complicated than first-trimester abortions and are performed only in certain hospitals. Early detection of pregnancy and accurate gestational dating allow for earlier presentation for abortions, hence a decrease in the cost of travelling to distant hospitals. Information on accessing pregnancy testing should be widely disseminated. In addition, working with and training community health workers so that they can assist women in estimating their gestational age from the last menstrual period may be useful.

INDIVIDUAL SYMBOLIC DIMENSION

Understanding individual lived experiences of unwanted and unsupportable pregnancies and of abortion. Locating these experiences within the social and structural dynamics of particular contexts, especially in service and training.

Sometimes only one conversation with someone in a difficult situation is needed to initiate empathy towards that person, especially if the general circumstances of the two are similar. During some of the interviews, participants expressed empathy towards women seeking abortions, speaking of what their choices might be in such a situation despite not having been required to do so by the interviewers. Some participants lamented their lack of empathy towards women who had abortions and bemoaned the tendency to gossip and judge within their communities. Some participants who started off hard-line anti-abortion showed less judgement towards the end of the interview, despite the neutrality of the interview questions.

The CTOP Act follows a rights-based approach. While it is important to emphasise the right of a woman to decide the outcome of her pregnancy, a solely rights-based approach will likely have little traction in communities that are strongly pronatalist and often anti-abortion. Participants indicated that their community members would generally accept the choice to have an abortion where such a decision is underpinned by poverty, being unwed, being young, violence in the family or sexual violence. Stories highlighting how abortion decision making is located within particular circumstances and that women tend to make decisions based on the principles of care could be useful in extending the acceptability of abortion in these communities.[26]

Several negative gender dynamics operate in the communities in which data were collected. As has been found in research conducted in the Eastern Cape by other members of our research unit, paternity denial, partner abandonment and lack of partner support during pregnancy were mentioned frequently by participants in our study.[27]

Although rape was seen by many participants as an acceptable reason to terminate a pregnancy, several exceptions and caveats were evident in the data. These included that the foetus was not to blame for the rape (and therefore, the pregnancy should not be terminated); the woman was probably to blame for the rape (rape myths); and the woman should simply endure the emotional fallout from the rape. If the rape assailant was known to the woman, abortion was seen as less acceptable. Additional reasons were seen as needed for rape to be an acceptable reason to terminate the pregnancy. These included that the woman may hate the child; the child would be disabled; fatherless children are problematic; and significant trauma was attached to the rape.

Conjugalised pronatalism, in which ideal womanhood is associated with being married and bearing children, is firmly entrenched in these communities. Married women who terminate a pregnancy are particularly judged.

Equally troubling were stories of abortion coercion, in which families or partners would overtly or covertly pressure women into having an abortion. Some of these stories had to do with the extension to the family of shame and stigma resulting from a socially inappropriate pregnancy. Other accounts were related to poverty. Addressing these kinds of dynamics in a sensitive, contextually relevant manner through outreach services and in collaboration with local NGOs would be a useful reproductive health intervention.

Katrina Kimport et al. argue that abortion support talklines can provide a certain level of encouragement and understanding to women who want to discuss their abortion experiences.[28] Other post-abortion support-focused programmes have created a safe space for women to disclose their abortions.[29] These kinds of spaces can assist women in gaining confidence in their decision.[30] Once again, however, these groups need to be confidential, and their specific aim of speaking about abortion in a rural area needs to be dealt with carefully.

The continued use of illegal and unsafe abortion services is of great public health concern in South Africa. Many writers have addressed the phenomenon whereby liberal abortion laws, such as those in South Africa, have not significantly decreased the use of unsafe abortion services and practices.[31] Our findings suggest that the history and knowledge of the adverse effects of unsafe abortions have influenced how abortions are perceived as akin to suicidal behaviour.

STRENGTHS AND LIMITATIONS OF THE STUDY

The Eastern Cape is particularly affected by poverty and lack of access to resources. Our study results may or may not be generalisable to similar provinces in South Africa. Nevertheless, the fact that we sampled across three different rural settings means that some of the diversity evident in rural communities in South Africa has been captured. Findings common across the settings may be generalisable to other rural communities within the country.

The use of one-on-one interviews in this study may limit the extent to which community perspectives on abortion-seeking behaviours and preferences were obtained. However, understanding participants as key informants who report on community perspectives may diminish this limitation, particularly as the qualitative component was designed to ensure that participants knew they were understood as key informants. Furthermore, one-on-one interviews offer greater privacy and confidentiality, which may decrease the likelihood of discomfort when discussing sensitive topics. Studies have noted that participants may find it difficult to speak about abortion.[32] In our study, this challenge was mitigated to some extent by asking participants to reflect on community views and understandings instead of their own views.

Reimbursement for participation in research is a contentious issue. In resource-poor areas where reimbursement is offered, ethics debates hinge on the ability of participants to refuse consent to participate, on the one hand, and the need to acknowledge the time spent or to reimburse costs incurred by participating in the study, on the other. In resource-poor or impoverished settings, substantial reimbursement may greatly reduce the likelihood that individuals will refuse to participate in the study and is therefore considered unethical.[33] These considerations featured in our research as well. For the DCE component of the study, the fieldworkers consisted of the home-based carers employed by the partner NGOs in the remote village and rural town. In consultation with the NGOs, we did not directly compensate the home-based carers but instead provided money to the NGOs' budgets to employ these workers. We provided a token of appreciation to research participants for their involvement in the qualitative section of the study, as the time commitment was substantial. This took the form of airtime or data worth R100 sent to their mobile phones.

FINAL CONCLUSIONS

There is a real possibility for reproductive justice to be served if safe and quality abortion care is extended to South Africans living in rural areas. Providing abortion services in these areas is challenging and, as this study shows, will require some changes in the current approach to abortion service provision, as well as – and most importantly – political will on the part of the South African government. The attitude with which government officials and employees, from the top level of government to nurses and health workers, approach the provision of abortion services impacts the general acceptance of abortion. As this study shows, abortion stigma plays a vital role in people's access to this important reproductive right. Moreover, if abortion services are provided in rural areas in a non-judgmental way, rural abortion clinics and providers could become vehicles towards full attainment of reproductive health and rights in rural South Africa, contributing towards a broader agenda of women's equality and liberty.

NOTES

INTRODUCTION: SETTING THE SCENE

1   Quoted in Tiyese Jeranji, 'Navigating Abortion Barriers in Rural Areas', *Spotlight*, 12 February 2021, https://www.spotlightnsp.co.za/2021/02/12/navigating-abortion-barriers-in-rural-areas/ (accessed 4 July 2022).

2   Jeranji, 'Navigating Abortion Barriers'.

3   Republic of South Africa, Choice on Termination of Pregnancy Act No. 92 (1996), https://www.gov.za/documents/choice-termination-pregnancy-act (accessed 13 June 2023); Republic of South Africa, Choice on Termination of Pregnancy Amendment Act No. 1 (2008), https://www.gov.za/sites/default/files/gcis_document/201409/a1-08.pdf (accessed 13 June 2023).

4   Sally Guttmacher et al., 'Abortion Reform in South Africa: A Case Study of the 1996 Choice on Termination of Pregnancy Act', *International Perspectives on Sexual and Reproductive Health* 24, no. 4 (1998), https://doi.org/10.2307/2991980.

5   Republic of South Africa, Choice on Termination of Pregnancy Act No. 92, preamble.

6   Republic of South Africa, Choice on Termination of Pregnancy Amendment Act No. 1.

7   Kim Eva Dickson et al., 'Abortion Service Provision in South Africa Three Years after Liberalization of the Law', *Studies in Family Planning* 34, no. 4 (2003), https://doi.org/10.1111/j.1728-4465.2003.00277.x; Rachel K. Jewkes et al., 'Why Are Women Still Aborting Outside Designated Facilities in Metropolitan South Africa?' *BJOG: An International Journal of Obstetrics & Gynaecology* 112, no. 9 (2005), https://doi.org/10.1111/j.1471-0528.2005.00697.x.

8   Jane Harries et al., 'Delays in Seeking an Abortion until the Second Trimester: A Qualitative Study in South Africa', *Reproductive Health* 4, no. 7 (2007), https://doi.org/10.1186/1742-4755-4-7; Jane Harries, Kathryn Stinson and Phyllis Orner, 'Health Care Providers' Attitudes towards Termination of Pregnancy: A Qualitative Study in South Africa', *BMC Public Health* 9, no. 1 (2009), https://doi.org/10.1186/1471-2458-9-296.

9   Greta Alice Bertolè, 'Abortion in South Africa: The Consequences of Conscientious Objection', *LSE International Development Review* 1, no. 2 (2021),

https://idr.lse.ac.uk/articles/abstract/33/ (accessed 15 March 2022); Jane Harries et al., 'Conscientious Objection and Its Impact on Abortion Service Provision in South Africa: A Qualitative Study', *Reproductive Health* 11, no. 1 (2014), https://doi.org/10.1186/1742-4755-11-16; Karen A. Trueman and Makgoale Magwentshu, 'Abortion in a Progressive Legal Environment: The Need for Vigilance in Protecting and Promoting Access to Safe Abortion Services in South Africa', *American Journal of Public Health* 103, no. 3 (2013), https://ajph.aphapublications.org/doi/full/10.2105/AJPH.2012.301194.

10   Chris Bateman, 'Abortion Practices Undermining Reformist Laws – Experts: Izindaba', *South African Medical Journal* 101, no. 5 (2011), https://journals.co.za/content/m_samj/101/5/EJC67589 (accessed 11 July 2022).

11   Caitlin Gerdts et al., 'Denial of Abortion in Legal Settings', *Journal of Family Planning and Reproductive Health Care* 41, no. 3 (2015), https://doi.org/10.1136/jfprhc-2014-100999.

12   Harries et al., 'Delays in Seeking an Abortion'.

13   Phyllis Orner, Maria de Bruyn and Diane Cooper, '"It Hurts, but I Don't Have a Choice, I'm Not Working and I'm Sick": Decisions and Experiences Regarding Abortion of Women Living with HIV in Cape Town, South Africa', *Culture, Health and Sexuality* 13, no. 7 (2011), https://doi.org/10.1080/13691058.2011.577907.

14   Rachel K. Jewkes and Helen Rees, 'Dramatic Decline in Abortion Mortality Due to the Choice on Termination of Pregnancy Act', *South African Medical Journal* 95, no. 4 (2005); Catriona Ida Macleod and Tiffany Tracey, 'Pregnancy among Young Women in South Africa,' in *International Handbook of Adolescent Pregnancy: Medical, Psychosocial, and Public Health Responses*, ed. Andrew Cherry and Mary Dillon (Boston: Springer, 2014), https://doi.org/10.1007/978-1-4899-8026-7_30.

15   Jewkes and Rees, 'Dramatic Decline'.

16   Jennifer Moodley and Victor Shola Akinsooto, 'Unsafe Abortions in a Developing Country: Has Liberalisation of Laws on Abortions Made a Difference?' *African Journal of Reproductive Health* 7, no. 2 (2003), https://doi.org/10.2307/3583211.

17   Deborah Constant et al., 'Self-Induction of Abortion among Women Accessing Second-Trimester Abortion Services in the Public Sector, Western Cape Province, South Africa: An Exploratory Study', *South African Medical Journal* 104, no. 4 (2014), https://doi.org/10.7196/SAMJ.7408.

18   Rebecca Hodes, 'The Culture of Illegal Abortion in South Africa', *Journal of Southern African Studies* 42, no. 1 (2016), https://doi.org/10.1080/03057070.2016.1133086; Ramprakash Kaswa, George F.D. Rupesinghe and Benjamin Longo-Mbenza, 'Exploring the Pregnant Women's Perspective of Late Booking of Antenatal Care Services at Mbekweni Health Centre in Eastern Cape, South Africa', *African Journal of Primary Health Care & Family Medicine* 10, no. 1 (2018), https://doi.org/10.4102/phcfm.v10i1.1300.

19   Cathi Albertyn, 'Claiming and Defending Abortion Rights in South Africa', *Revista Direito GV* 11, no. 2 (2015), https://doi.org/10.1590/1808-2432201519.

20   Orner, De Bruyn and Cooper, '"It Hurts"'.

21   Amnesty International, 'Barriers to Safe and Legal Abortion in South Africa', 1 February 2017, https://www.amnesty.org/en/documents/afr53/5423/2017/en/ (accessed 22 February 2022).

22   Both the full and short reports can be found at https://www.ru.ac.za/criticalstudies/booksandpublications/reports/.

23　Helen Bradford, 'Herbs, Knives and Plastic: 150 Years of Abortion in South Africa', in *Science, Medicine and Cultural Imperialism*, ed. Teresa Meade and Mark Walker (London: Palgrave Macmillan, 1991), https://doi.org/10.1007/978-1-349-12445-9_7; George Devereux, *A Study of Abortion in Primitive Societies* (New York: International Universities Press, 1976).

24　Bradford, 'Herbs, Knives and Plastic'; Catherine Burns, 'Controlling Birth: Johannesburg, 1920–1960', *South African Historical Journal* 50, no. 1 (2004), https://doi.org/10.1080/02582470409464801; Rebecca Hodes, 'The Medical History of Abortion in South Africa, c. 1970–2000', *Journal of Southern African Studies* 39, no. 3 (2013), https://doi.org/10.1080/03057070.2013.824770; Susanne M. Klausen, *Abortion under Apartheid: Nationalism, Sexuality, and Women's Reproductive Rights in South Africa, 1919–1939* (Oxford: Oxford University Press, 2015), https://doi.org/10.1017/CBO9781107415324.004; Susanne M. Klausen, *Race, Maternity, and the Politics of Birth Control in South Africa, 1910–39* (Houndmills: Palgrave Macmillan, 2004); Susanne M. Klausen, '"The Trial the World Is Watching": The 1972 Prosecution of Derk Crichton and James Watts, Abortion, and the Regulation of the Medical Profession in Apartheid South Africa', *Medical History* 58, no. 2 (2014), https://doi.org/10.1017/mdh.2014.6.

25　John W. de Gruchy, 'Calvin(ism) and Apartheid in South Africa in the Twentieth Century: The Making and Unmaking of a Racial Ideology', in *Calvin and His Influence, 1509–2009*, ed. Irena Backus and Philip Benedict (Oxford: Oxford University Press, 2011), https://doi.org/10.1093/acprof:oso/9780199751846.003.0016.

26　Republic of South Africa, Prohibition of Mixed Marriages Act No. 55 (1949), https://en.wikisource.org/wiki/Prohibition_of_Mixed_Marriages_Act,_1949 (accessed 13 June 2023).

27　Republic of South Africa, Immorality Amendment Act No. 21 (1950), https://en.wikisource.org/wiki/Immorality_Amendment_Act,_1950 (accessed 13 June 2023).

28　Republic of South Africa, Population Registration Act No. 30 (1950), https://en.wikisource.org/wiki/Population_Registration_Act,_1950 (accessed 13 June 2023).

29　Republic of South Africa, Immorality Amendment Act No. 57 (1969), https://www.gov.za/sites/default/files/gcis_document/201505/act-57-1969.pdf (accessed 13 June 2023).

30　Klausen, *Abortion under Apartheid*.

31　Hodes, 'Medical History of Abortion'.

32　Klausen, *Abortion under Apartheid*, 25.

33　Klausen, *Race, Maternity, and the Politics*.

34　Hodes, 'Medical History of Abortion'.

35　Klausen, *Abortion under Apartheid*.

36　Republic of South Africa, Abortion and Sterilization Act No. 2 (1975), https://www.lexisnexis.co.za/__data/assets/pdf_file/0020/820325/Abortion-and-Sterilization-Act-No.-2-of-1975.pdf (accessed 15 June 2023).

37　Helen Rees, 'The Abortion Debate in South Africa', *Newsletter: Women's Global Network on Reproductive Rights*, no. 36 (July–September 1991).

38　Rees, 'Abortion Debate'.

39   Klausen, *Abortion under Apartheid*.

40   Hodes, 'Medical History of Abortion'.

41   Hodes, 'Medical History of Abortion'.

42   Daniel Grossman et al., 'Medication Abortion with Pharmacist Dispensing of Mifepristone', *Obstetrics and Gynecology* 137, no. 4 (2021): 613, https://doi.org/10.1097/AOG.0000000000004312.

43   Harries et al., 'Delays in Seeking an Abortion'.

44   Lewis Dijkstra, Ellen Hamilton and Sameh Wahba, 'How Do We Define Cities, Towns, and Rural Areas?', *World Bank Blogs: Sustainable Cities*, 10 March 2020, https://blogs.worldbank.org/sustainablecities/how-do-we-define-cities-towns-and-rural-areas (accessed 14 July 2022).

45   Sharthi Laldaparsad, 'Urban and Rural Trends in South Africa', in *Proceedings of the 59th World Statistics Congress of the International Statistical Institute* (The Hague: ISI, 2013).

46   Michael Clark and Nolundi Luwaya, 'Communal Land Tenure 1994–2017: Commissioned Report for High Level Panel on the Assessment of Key Legislation and the Acceleration of Fundamental Change, an Initiative of the Parliament of South Africa', June 2017, Land and Accountability Research Unit, University of Cape Town, 3.

47   Laldaparsad, 'Urban and Rural Trends'.

48   Laldaparsad, 'Urban and Rural Trends'.

49   Johannes Tsheola, 'Paradoxes of Gendered Rurality, Women's Non-Economic Constructions, Disempowerment and State Capitalism in South Africa', *Academic Journal of Interdisciplinary Studies* 3, no. 1 (2014): 315, https://doi.org/10.5901/ajis.2014.v3n1p315.

50   Kara Grace Mackay, 'Who Sits at the Table? A Female Farm Activist's Experience during the De Doorns Farm Workers Strike, South Africa', *Revista Brasileira de Educação Do Campo* 3, no. 3 (2018), https://doi.org/10.20873/uft.2525-4863.2018v3n3p937.

51   Katherine S. Nelson et al., 'Definitions, Measures, and Uses of Rurality: A Systematic Review of the Empirical and Quantitative Literature', *Journal of Rural Studies* 82 (February 2021), https://doi.org/10.1016/j.jrurstud.2021.01.035.

52   Greg Ruiters, ed., *The Fate of the Eastern Cape: History, Politics and Social Policy* (Pietermaritzburg: University of KwaZulu-Natal Press, 2011).

53   Statistics South Africa, 'Living Conditions of Households in South Africa: An Analysis of Household Expenditure and Income Data Using the LCS 2014/2015', Statistical Release P0310, 2017, https://www.statssa.gov.za/publications/P0310/P03102014.pdf (accessed 21 June 2022).

54   http://ecarp.org.za/.

55   https://keiskamma.org/.

56   https://bulungulaincubator.org/.

57   James Drisko and Tina Maschi, *Content Analysis* (Oxford: Oxford University Press, 2016).

58   Esther W. de Bekker-Grob, 'Discrete Choice Experiments in Health Care' (PhD thesis, Erasmus University, Rotterdam, 2009), https://doi.org/10.1136/bmj.328.7436.360.

59   John F.P. Bridges et al., 'Conjoint Analysis Applications in Health – a Checklist: A Report of the ISPOR Good Research Practices for Conjoint Analysis Task Force', *Value in Health* 14, no. 4 (2011) https://doi.org/10.1016/j.jval.2010.11.013.

60   DEDEAT (Department of Economic Development, Environmental Affairs and Tourism), 'The Eastern Cape Socio-Economic Review and Outlook', 2017, https://ecsecc.org/infocentre (accessed 21 September 2022).

61   Available at https://www.ru.ac.za/media/rhodesuniversity/content/criticalstudi esinsexualitiesandreproduction/documents/CSSR_-_MSSA_Study_Research_Report_-_2020.pdf.

62   Loretta J. Ross and Rickie Solinger, *Reproductive Justice* (Berkeley: University of California Press, (2017).

63   Tracy Morison, 'Reproductive Justice: A Radical Framework for Researching Sexual and Reproductive Issues in Psychology', *Social and Personality Psychology Compass* 15, no. 6 (2021), https://doi.org/10.1111/spc3.12605; Tracy Morison and Jabulile Mary-Jane Jace Mavuso, eds., *Reproductive Justice: From the Margins to the Centre* (Lanham: Lexington Press, 2022).

CHAPTER 1: 'IF IT IS LEGAL THESE DAYS, I DO NOT KNOW'

1   Cecilia Espinoza, Ghazaleh Samandari and Kathryn Andersen, 'Abortion Knowledge, Attitudes and Experiences among Adolescent Girls: A Review of the Literature', *Sexual and Reproductive Health Matters* 28, no. 1 (2020), https://doi.org/10.1080/26410397.2020.1744225.

2   Frances A. Althaus, 'Work in Progress: The Expansion of Access to Abortion Services in South Africa Following Legalization', *International Family Planning Perspectives* 26, no. 3 (2000), https://doi.org/10.2307/2648272.

3   Chelsea Morroni, Landon Myer and Kemilembe Tibazarwa, 'Knowledge of the Abortion Legislation among South African Women: A Cross-Sectional Study', *Reproductive Health* 3, no. 1 (2006), https://doi.org/10.1186/1742-4755-3-7.

4   Kelvin Mwaba and Pamela Naidoo, 'Knowledge, Beliefs and Attitudes Regarding Abortion in South Africa among a Sample of University Students', *Journal of Psychology in Africa* 16, no. 1 (2006), https://doi.org/10.1080/14330237.2006.1082 0104.

5   Catriona Ida Macleod, Lebogang Seutlwadi and Gary Steele, 'Cracks in Reproductive Health Rights: Buffalo City Learners' Knowledge of Abortion Legislation', *Health SA Gesondheid* 19, no. 1 (2014), https://doi.org/10.4102/hsag.v19i1.743.

6   Devashnee Ramiyad and Cynthia J. Patel, 'Exploring South African Adolescents' Knowledge of Abortion Legislation and Attitudes to Abortion: Sexual Status and Gender Differences', *South African Journal of Child Health* 10, no. 2 (2016), https://doi.org/10.7196/sajch.2016.v10i2.1137.

7   Participants were given pseudonyms.

8   Ramiyad and Patel, 'Exploring South African Adolescents' Knowledge'.

9   Macleod, Seutlwadi and Steele, 'Cracks in Reproductive Health Rights'.

10   Mary Favier, Jamie M.S. Greenberg and Marion Stevens, 'Safe Abortion in South Africa: "We Have Wonderful Laws but We Don't Have People to Implement Those Laws"', *International Journal of Gynecology and Obstetrics* 143, suppl. 4 (October 2018), https://doi.org/10.1002/ijgo.12676.

11   Joan van Dyk, 'Need an Abortion? Find Clinics You Can Trust Here', *Mail & Guardian*, 24 November 2021, https://mg.co.za/health/2021-11-24-need-an-abortion-find-clinics-you-can-trust-here/ (accessed 18 July 2022).

12   Available at: https://wheretocare.org/.
13   Macleod, Seutlwadi and Steele, 'Cracks in Reproductive Health Rights'.
14   Marie E. Sullivan et al., 'Women's Reproductive Decision Making and Abortion Experiences in Cape Town, South Africa: A Qualitative Study', *Health Care for Women International* 39, no. 11 (2018), https://doi.org/10.1080/07399332.2017.140 0034.
15   Harries et al., 'Conscientious Objection'.
16   Jabulile Mary-Jane Jace Mavuso and Catriona Ida Macleod, '"Bad Choices": Unintended Pregnancy and Abortion in Nurses and Counsellors' Accounts of Providing Pre-Abortion Counselling', *Health* 25, no. 5 (2021): 570 (italics in original), https://doi.org/10.1177/1363459320988873.
17   Joanna N. Erdman, Kinga Jelinska and Susan Yanow, 'Understandings of Self-Managed Abortion as Health Inequity, Harm Reduction and Social Change', *Reproductive Health Matters* 26, no. 54 (2018), https://www.jstor.org/stable/26605082 (accessed 24 July 2022).
18   Mariana Prandini Assis and Sara Larrea, 'Why Self-Managed Abortion Is So Much More than a Provisional Solution for Times of Pandemic', *Sexual and Reproductive Health Matters* 28, no. 1 (2020), https://doi.org/10.1080/26410397.2020.1779633.
19   Caitlin Gerdts et al., 'Women's Experiences Seeking Informal Sector Abortion Services in Cape Town, South Africa: A Descriptive Study', *BMC Women's Health* 17, no. 95 (2017), https://doi.org/10.1186/s12905-017-0443-6.
20   Jane Harries et al., 'An Exploratory Study of What Happens to Women Who Are Denied Abortions in Cape Town, South Africa', *Reproductive Health* 12, no. 1 (2015): 4, https://doi.org/10.1186/s12978-015-0014-y.
21   Harries et al., 'Delays in Seeking an Abortion'.
22   Maria de Bruyn, 'Women, Reproductive Rights, and HIV/AIDS: Issues on Which Research and Interventions Are Still Needed', *Journal of Health, Population and Nutrition* 24, no. 4 (2006), https://api.semanticscholar.org/CorpusID:19951069.
23   Constancia Mavodza, Rebecca Goldman and Bergen Cooper, 'The Impacts of the Global Gag Rule on Global Health: A Scoping Review', *Global Health Research and Policy* 4, no. 26 (2019), https://doi.org/10.1186/s41256-019-0113-3.

CHAPTER 2: ABORTING A PREGNANCY

1   Republic of South Africa, Choice on Termination of Pregnancy Act No. 92, preamble.
2   Malvern Chiweshe, Jabulile Mavuso and Catriona Ida Macleod, 'Reproductive Justice in Context: South African and Zimbabwean Women's Narratives of Their Abortion Decision', *Feminism & Psychology* 27, no. 2 (2017), https://doi.org/10.1177/0959353517699234; Mabel L.S. Lie, Stephen C. Robson and Carl R. May, 'Experiences of Abortion: A Narrative Review of Qualitative Studies', *BMC Health Services Research* 8, no. 150 (2008), https://doi.org/10.1186/1472-6963-8-150.
3   Harries et al., 'Delays in Seeking an Abortion'.
4   Sullivan et al., 'Women's Reproductive Decision Making', 1170.
5   Catriona Macleod, Sibongile Matebese and Nontozamo Tsetse, '"I Drank Because I Wanted to Deal with the Frustration": Explaining Alcohol Consumption during Pregnancy in a Low-Resource Setting – Women's, Partners' and Family

Members' Narratives', *Social Work* 56, no. 1 (2020), https://doi.org/10.15270/52-2-792; Sibongile Matebese, Catriona Ida Macleod and Nontozamo Tsetse, 'The Shame of Drinking Alcohol While Pregnant: The Production of Avoidance and Ill Health', *Journal of Women and Social Work* 36, no. 4 (2021), https://doi.org/10.1177/0886109920985139.

6   Elizabeth Price et al., 'Experiences of Reproductive Coercion in Queensland Women', *Journal of Interpersonal Violence* 37, no. 5–6 (2022): NP2825, https://doi.org/10.1177/0886260519846851.

7   Chiweshe, Mavuso and Macleod, 'Reproductive Justice in Context'.

8   Esona Bottoman, 'Pregnant Women's Construction of Social Support from Their Intimate Partners during Pregnancy' (Master's thesis, Rhodes University, 2018), http://vital.seals.ac.za:8080/vital/access/manager/Repository/vital:28207, accessed 26 March 2022.

9   Bottoman, 'Pregnant Women's Construction'.

10   Sisa Ngabaza, 'Positively Pregnant: Teenage Women's Experiences of Negotiating Pregnancy with Their Families', *Agenda: Empowering Women for Gender Equity* 25, no. 3 (2011): 42, https://doi.org/10.1080/10130950.2011.610985.

11   Michalinos Zembylas, '"Shame at Being Human" as a Transformative Political Concept and Praxis: Pedagogical Possibilities', *Feminism and Psychology* 29, no. 2 (2019), https://doi.org/10.1177/0959353518754592.

12   Zembylas, '"Shame at Being Human"'.

13   Tamara Shefer, Deevia Bhana and Robert Morrell, 'Teenage Pregnancy and Parenting at School in Contemporary South African Contexts: Deconstructing School Narratives and Understanding Policy Implementation', *Perspectives in Education* 31, no. 1 (2013): 1.

14   Lauren Ralph et al., 'The Role of Parents and Partners in Minors' Decisions to Have an Abortion and Anticipated Coping after Abortion', *Journal of Adolescent Health* 54, no. 4 (2014), https://doi.org/10.1016/j.jadohealth.2013.09.021.

15   Republic of South Africa, Choice on Termination of Pregnancy Act No. 92, section 2(1)(b)(iv).

16   Diana Greene Foster, *The Turnaway Study: Ten Years, a Thousand Women, and the Consequences of Having – or Being Denied – an Abortion* (New York: Scribner, 2020).

17   Tracey Feltham-King and Catriona Ida Macleod, 'Multi-Layered Risk Management in Under-Resourced Antenatal Clinics: A Scientific-Bureaucratic Approach versus Street-Level Bureaucracy', *Health, Risk & Society* 22, no. 1 (2020), https://doi.org/10.1080/13698575.2019.1697432.

18   Joy Ebonwu et al., 'Determinants of Late Antenatal Care Presentation in Rural and Peri-Urban Communities in South Africa: A Cross-Sectional Study', *PLOS ONE* 13, no. 3 (2018), https://doi.org/10.1371/journal.pone.0191903.

19   Rachelle Joy Chadwick, 'Obstetric Violence in South Africa', *South African Medical Journal* 106, no. 5 (2016).

20   Chiweshe, Mavuso and Macleod, 'Reproductive Justice in Context'.

21   Rachel K. Jones, Lori F. Frohwirth and Ann M. Moore, '"I Would Want to Give My Child, like, Everything in the World": How Issues of Motherhood Influence Women Who Have Abortions', *Journal of Family Issues* 29, no. 1 (2007), https://doi.org/10.1177/0192513X07305753.

22 Saara Greene, 'Becoming Responsible: Young Mothers' Decision-Making Regarding Motherhood and Abortion', *Journal of Progressive Human Services* 17, no. 1 (2006), https://doi.org/10.1300/J059v17n01.

23 Chimaraoke O. Izugbaraa, Rhoune Ochako and Chibuogwu Izugbara, 'Gender Scripts and Unwanted Pregnancy among Urban Kenyan Women', *Culture, Health and Sexuality* 13, no. 9 (2011), https://doi.org/10.1080/13691058.2011.598947.

24 Chadwick, 'Obstetric Violence', 423.

CHAPTER 3: SIN, INJURY AND DISCORD

1 Abigail Harrison et al., 'Barriers to Implementing South Africa's Termination of Pregnancy Act in Rural KwaZulu/Natal', *Health Policy and Planning* 15, no. 4 (2000).

2 Mwaba and Naidoo, 'Knowledge, Beliefs and Attitudes'.

3 Cynthia J. Patel and Trisha Kooverjee, 'Abortion and Contraception: Attitudes of South African University Students', *Health Care for Women International* 30, no. 6 (2009), https://doi.org/10.1080/07399330902886105.

4 Tracey Feltham-King and Catriona Ida Macleod, 'Gender, Abortion and Substantive Representation in the South African Newsprint Media', *Women's Studies International Forum* 51 (2015), https://doi.org/10.1016/j.wsif.2015.04.001; Catriona Ida Macleod and Jateen Hansjee, 'Men and Talk about Legal Abortion in South Africa: Equality, Support and Rights Discourses Undermining Reproductive "Choice"', *Culture, Health & Sexuality* 15, no. 8 (2013), https://doi.org/10.1080/136 91058.2013.802815.

5 Lebohang Selebalo-Bereng and Cynthia Joan Patel, 'Reasons for Abortion: Religion, Religiosity/Spirituality and Attitudes of Male Secondary School Youth in South Africa', *Journal of Religion and Health* 58, no. 6 (2019), https://doi.org/10.1007/s10943-017-0547-1.

6 Kristin Luker, *Abortion and the Politics of Motherhood* (Berkeley: University of California Press, 1984).

7 Anuradha Kumar, 'Disgust, Stigma, and the Politics of Abortion', *Feminism and Psychology* 28, no. 4 (2018): 534, https://doi.org/10.1177/0959353518765572.

8 Government of Ireland, Health (Regulation of Termination of Pregnancy) Act No. 31 of 2018, https://www.irishstatutebook.ie/eli/2018/act/31 (accessed 15 June 2023).

9 Kumar, 'Disgust, Stigma'.

10 Radhamany Sooryamoorthy and Mzwandile Makhoba, 'The Family in Modern South Africa: Insights from Recent Research', *Journal of Comparative Family Studies* 47, no. 3 (2016).

11 Alexa J. Trumpy, 'Woman vs. Fetus: Frame Transformation and Intramovement Dynamics in the Pro-Life Movement', *Sociological Spectrum* 34, no. 2 (2014), https://doi.org/10.1080/02732173.2014.878624.

12 Tracy Morison, 'Heterosexual Men and Parenthood Decision Making in South Africa: Attending to the Invisible Norm', *Qualitative Research* 34, no. 8 (2013), https://doi.org/10.1177/0192513X13484271.

13 World Health Organization, 'Abortion', 25 November 2021, https://www.who.int/news-room/fact-sheets/detail/abortion (accessed 17 July 2022).

14 Sam Rowlands, 'Misinformation on Abortion', *European Journal of Contraception & Reproductive Health Care* 16, no. 4 (2011): 233, doi: 10.3109/13625187.2011.570883.
15 Rowlands, 'Misinformation'.
16 Chiweshe, Mavuso and Macleod, 'Reproductive Justice in Context'.
17 Lisa Vetten et al., 'Tracking Justice: The Attrition of Rape Cases through the Criminal Justice System in Gauteng', Tshwaranang Legal Advocacy Centre, the South African Medical Research Council and the Centre for the Study of Violence and Reconciliation, 2008, https://www.csvr.org.za/tracking-justice-the-attrition-of-rape-cases-through-the-criminal-justice-system-in-gauteng/ (accessed 1 August 2022).
18 Sophie Sills et al., 'Rape Culture and Social Media: Young Critics and a Feminist Counterpublic', *Feminist Media Studies* 16, no. 6 (2016), https://doi.org/10.1080/14 680777.2015.1137962.
19 Catriona Ida Macleod, *'Adolescence', Pregnancy and Abortion: Constructing a Threat of Degeneration* (London: Routledge, 2011); Catriona Ida Macleod and Tracey Feltham-King, '"Adolescent Pregnancy": Social Problem, Public Health Concern, or Neither?' in *Routledge International Handbook of Women's Sexual and Reproductive Health*, ed. Jane Ussher, Joan Chrisler and Janette Perz (Abingdon: Routledge, 2019), https://doi.org/10.4324/9781351035620-17.
20 Catriona Ida Macleod and Tiffany Tracey, 'A Decade Later: Follow-up Review of South African Research on the Consequences of and Contributory Factors in Teen-aged Pregnancy', *South African Journal of Psychology* 40, no. 1 (2010), https://doi.org/10.1177/008124631004000103.
21 Macleod, *'Adolescence'*.
22 Robert Morrell, Deevia Bhana and Tamara Shefer, eds., *Books and Babies: Pregnancy and Young Parents in Schools* (Cape Town: HSRC Press, 2012).
23 John B. Pryor, Glenn D. Reeder and Andrew E. Monroe, 'The Infection of Bad Company: Stigma by Association', *Journal of Personality and Social Psychology* 102, no. 2 (2012): 224, https://doi.org/10.1037/a0026270.
24 Macleod, *'Adolescence'*.

CHAPTER 4: 'AND THE STORY SPREAD'

1 Anuradha Kumar, Leila Hessini and Ellen M.H. Mitchell, 'Conceptualising Abortion Stigma', *Culture, Health & Sexuality* 11, no. 6, https://doi.org/10.1080/13691050902842741; Alison Norris et al., 'Abortion Stigma: A Reconceptualization of Constituents, Causes, and Consequences', *Women's Health Issues* 21, suppl. 3 (2011), https://doi.org/https://doi.org/10.1016/j.whi.2011.02.010; Kristen M. Shellenberg and Amy O. Tsui, 'Correlates of Perceived and Internalized Stigma among Abortion Patients in the USA: An Exploration by Race and Hispanic Ethnicity', *International Journal of Gynecology and Obstetrics* 118, suppl. 2 (2012), https://doi.org/10.1016/S0020-7292(12)60015-0.
2 Kate Cockrill et al., 'The Stigma of Having an Abortion: Development of a Scale and Characteristics of Women Experiencing Abortion Stigma', *Perspectives on Sexual and Reproductive Health* 45, no. 2 (2013), https://doi.org/10.1363/4507913.
3 Kumar, Hessini and Mitchell, 'Conceptualising Abortion Stigma', 628.

4   Erving Goffman, *Stigma: Notes on the Management of Spoiled Identity* (Englewood Cliffs, N.J: Prentice-Hall, 1963).

5   Goffman, *Stigma*, 4.

6   Kate Cockrill and Adina Nack, '"I'm Not That Type of Person": Managing the Stigma of Having an Abortion', *Deviant Behavior* 34, no. 12 (2013): 975, https://doi.org/10.1080/01639625.2013.800423.

7   Jennifer L. Holland, 'Abolishing Abortion: The History of the Pro-Life Movement in America', *American Historian*, November 2016, https://www.oah.org/tah/issues/2016/november/abolishing-abortion-the-history-of-the-pro-life-movement-in-america/ (accessed 17 July 2022).

8   Kumar, Hessini and Mitchell, 'Conceptualising Abortion Stigma'.

9   Kumar, 'Disgust, Stigma'.

10 Bruce G. Link and Jo C. Phelan, 'Conceptualizing Stigma', *Annual Review of Sociology* 27, no. 1 (2001), https://doi.org/10.1146/annurev.soc.27.1.363.

11 Jonathan Bearak et al., 'Unintended Pregnancy and Abortion by Income, Region, and the Legal Status of Abortion: Estimates from a Comprehensive Model for 1990–2019', *The Lancet Global Health* 8, no. 9 (2020), https://doi.org/10.1016/S2214-109X(20)30315-6.

12 Guttmacher Institute, 'Abortion in Africa: Fact Sheet', March 2018, https://www.guttmacher.org/sites/default/files/factsheet/ib_aww-africa.pdf (accessed 15 July 2022).

13 Kumar, Hessini and Mitchell, 'Conceptualising Abortion Stigma', 629.

14 Link and Phelan, 'Conceptualizing Stigma'.

15 Carole Joffe, *Doctors of Conscience: The Struggle to Provide Abortion before and after Roe v. Wade* (Boston: Beacon Press, 1995).

16 Hodes, 'Culture of Illegal Abortion'.

17 Rachel Benson Gold and Elizabeth Nash, 'TRAP Laws Gain Political Traction While Abortion Clinics – and the Women They Serve – Pay the Price', *Guttmacher Policy Review* 16, no. 2 (2013), http://www.guttmacher.org/pubs/gpr/16/2/gpr160207.html (accessed 29 July 2022); Carol Joffe, *Dispatches from the Abortion Wars: The Costs of Fanaticism to Doctors, Patients and the Rest of Us* (Boston: Beacon Press, 2010); Jennefer A. Russo, Kristin L. Schumacher and Mitchell D. Creinin, 'Antiabortion Violence in the United States', *Contraception* 86, no. 5 (2012), https://doi.org/10.1016/j.contraception.2012.02.011.

18 Mary Fitzgerald, 'How US Anti-Abortion Groups Are Funding South Africa's "Pregnancy Crisis Centres"', Bhekisisa Centre for Journalism, 17 February 2020, https://bhekisisa.org/opinion/2020-02-17-how-us-anti-abortion-groups-are-funding-south-africas-pregnancy-crisis-centres/ (accessed 24 July 2022).

19 Jabulile Mavuso and Catriona Ida Macleod, 'Contradictions in Womxn's Experiences of Pre-Abortion Counselling in South Africa: Implications for Client-Centred Practice', *Nursing Inquiry* 27 no. 2 (2020), https://doi.org/10.1111/nin.12330.

20 Shellenberg and Tsui, 'Correlates'.

21 For example, Kristen M. Shellenberg et al., 'Social Stigma and Disclosure about Induced Abortion: Results from an Exploratory Study', *Global Public Health* 6, suppl. 1 (2011), https://doi.org/10.1080/17441692.2011.594072.

22 Link and Phelan, 'Conceptualizing Stigma'.

23 Cockrill and Nack, "'I'm Not That Type'".
24 Cockrill and Nack, "'I'm Not That Type'", 983.
25 Cockrill and Nack, "'I'm Not That Type'".
26 Cockrill and Nack, "'I'm Not That Type'".

CHAPTER 5: BARRIERS TO HAVING AN ABORTION IN RURAL SOUTH AFRICA

1 Catriona Ida Macleod, Malvern Chiweshe and Jabulile Mavuso, 'A Critical Review of Sanctioned Knowledge Production Concerning Abortion in Africa: Implications for Feminist Health Psychology', *Journal of Health Psychology* 23, no. 8 (July 2018), https://doi.org/10.1177/1359105316644294.
2 Harries et al., 'Delays in Seeking an Abortion'.
3 Naomi Lince-Deroche et al., 'Accessing Medical and Surgical First-Trimester Abortion Services: Women's Experiences and Costs from an Operations Research Study in KwaZulu-Natal Province, South Africa', *Contraception* 96, no. 2 (2017), https://doi.org/10.1016/j.contraception.2017.03.013.
4 Lorraine Greaves et al., 'From Fetal Health to Women's Health: Expanding the Gaze on Intervening on Smoking during Pregnancy', *Critical Public Health* 26, no. 2 (2016), https://doi.org/10.1080/09581596.2014.968527.
5 Kim Dickson-Tetteh and Deborah L. Billings, 'Abortion Care Services Provided by Registered Midwives in South Africa', *International Family Planning Perspectives* 28, no. 3 (2002), https://doi.org/10.2307/3088257.
6 Constant et al., 'Self-Induction of Abortion'.
7 Jane Harries and Deborah Constant, 'Providing Safe Abortion Services: Experiences and Perspectives of Providers in South Africa', *Best Practice and Research: Clinical Obstetrics and Gynaecology* 62 (January 2020): 80, https://doi.org/10.1016/j.bpobgyn.2019.05.005.
8 Harries, Stinson and Orner, 'Health Care Providers' Attitudes'.
9 Trueman and Magwentshu, 'Abortion in a Progressive Legal Environment'.
10 Harries et al., 'Delays in Seeking an Abortion'.
11 Harries et al., 'Delays in Seeking an Abortion'.
12 Harries et al., 'Delays in Seeking an Abortion'.
13 Rachel K. Jewkes et al., 'Prevalence of Morbidity Associated with Abortion before and after Legalisation in South Africa', *British Medical Journal* 324, no. 7348 (2002), https://doi.org/10.1136/bmj.324.7348.1252.
14 Rowlands, 'Misinformation', 233.
15 Chadwick, 'Obstetric Violence'.
16 Harries et al., 'Delays in Seeking an Abortion'.
17 Bateman, 'Abortion Practices'.
18 Ellen M.H. Mitchell et al., 'Building Alliances from Ambivalence: Evaluation of Abortion Values Clarification Workshops with Stakeholders in South Africa', *African Journal of Reproductive Health* 9, no. 3 (2005), https://doi.org/10.2307/3583415; Katherine L. Turner, Alyson G. Hyman and Mosotho C. Gabriel, 'Clarifying Values and Transforming Attitudes to Improve Access to Second Trimester Abortion', *Reproductive Health Matters* 16, suppl. 31 (2008), https://doi.org/10.1016/S0968-8080(08)31389-5.
19 Mavuso and Macleod, 'Contradictions'.

20   Laura Florence Harris et al., 'Conscientious Objection to Abortion Provision: Why Context Matters', *Global Public Health* 13, no. 5 (2018), https://doi.org/10.1080/174 41692.2016.1229353.

21   Christian Fiala and Joyce H. Arthur, '"Dishonourable Disobedience" – Why Refusal to Treat in Reproductive Healthcare Is Not Conscientious Objection', *Woman – Psychosomatic Gynaecology and Obstetrics* 1 (1 December 2014), https://doi.org/10.1016/J.WOMAN.2014.03.001.

22   Charles Ngwena, 'Conscientious Objection and Legal Abortion in South Africa: Delineating the Parameters', *Journal for Juridical Science* 28, no. 1 (2003), https://doi.org/10.4314/jjs.v28i1.27128.

23   Amnesty International, 'Barriers'.

24   Harries et al., 'Conscientious Objection'.

25   Hodes, 'Culture of Illegal Abortion'.

CONCLUSION: IMPLICATIONS AND FUTURE DIRECTIONS

1   Republic of South Africa, Choice on Termination of Pregnancy Act No. 92, 2 (italics added).

2   Amanda Dennis, Kelly Blanchard and Tshego Bessenaar, 'Identifying Indicators for Quality Abortion Care: A Systematic Literature Review', *Journal of Family Planning and Reproductive Health Care* 43, no. 1 (2017), https://doi.org/10.1136/jfprhc-2015-101427.

3   Catriona Ida Macleod, Siân Beynon-Jones and Merran Toerien, 'Articulating Reproductive Justice through Reparative Justice: Case Studies of Abortion in Great Britain and South Africa', *Culture, Health & Sexuality* 19, no. 5 (2017), https://doi.org /10.1080/13691058.2016.1257738; Catriona Ida Macleod and Tracey Feltham-King, 'Young Pregnant Women and Public Health: Introducing a Critical Reparative Justice/ Care Approach Using South African Case Studies', *Critical Public Health* 30, no. 3 (2020), https://doi.org/10.1080/09581596.2019.1573313; Catriona Ida Macleod and John Hunter Reynolds, 'Reproductive Health Systems Analyses and the Reparative Reproductive Justice Approach: A Case Study of Unsafe Abortion in Lesotho', *Global Public Health* 17, no. 6 (2021), https://doi.org/10.1080/17441692.2021.1887317.

4   Ross and Solinger, *Reproductive Justice*.

5   Robin DiAngelo and Özlem Sensoy, *Is Everyone Really Equal? An Introduction to Key Concepts in Social Justice Education*, 2nd ed. (New York: Teachers College Press, 2017), xix.

6   Ernesto Verdeja, 'A Critical Theory of Reparative Justice', *Constellations* 15, no. 2 (2008), https://doi.org/10.1111/j.1467-8675.2008.00485.x.; Macleod, Beynon-Jones and Toerien, 'Articulating Reproductive Justice'; Macleod and Feltham-King, 'Young Pregnant Women'; Macleod and Reynolds, 'Reproductive Health Systems Analyses'.

7   Frans Krüger, 'SA's Rich Bag of Big, Small and Eclectic Community Radio Stations', *University of the Witwatersrand News*, 16 February 2020, https://www.wits.ac.za/news/latest-news/opinion/2020/2020-02/sas-rich-bag-of-big-small-and-eclectic-community-radio-stations.html (accessed 28 September 2022).

8   Orner, De Bruyn and Cooper, '"It Hurts"'; Phyllis Orner, Maria de Bruyn and Diane Cooper, 'A Qualitative Exploration of HIV-Positive Pregnant Women's

Decision-Making Regarding Abortion in Cape Town, South Africa', *Methods* 7, no. 2 (2010).

9   Orner, De Bruyn and Cooper, '"It Hurts"'.

10 Gloria Nakajubi, 'Beware the Charlatan Sangomas', *Mail & Guardian*, 5 November 2015.

11 Mavuso and Macleod, '"Bad Choices"'.

12 Jabulile Mavuso et al., 'Abortion Counselling in South Africa: A Step-by-Step Guide for Providers', Critical Studies in Sexuality and Reproduction Research Unit, Rhodes University, 2018, https://srjc.org.za/wp-content/uploads/2017/06/Abortion_Counselling_Guide_Version_1-1.pdf (accessed 24 June 2023).

13 Cheryl Potgieter and Gail Andrews, 'South African Nurses' Accounts for Choosing to Be Termination of Pregnancy Providers', *Health SA Gesondheid* 9, no. 2 (2004), https://doi.org/10.4102/hsag.v9i2.161.

14 Kumar, Hessini and Mitchell, 'Conceptualising Abortion Stigma', 634.

15 Deeqa Mohamed, Nadia Diamond-Smith and Jesse Njunguru, 'Stigma and Agency: Exploring Young Kenyan Women's Experiences with Abortion Stigma and Individual Agency', *Reproductive Health Matters* 26, no. 52 (2018), https://doi.org/10.1080/09688080.2018.1492285.

16 Benjamin Elliot Yelnosky Smith et al., '"Without Any Indication": Stigma and a Hidden Curriculum within Medical Students' Discussion of Elective Abortion', *Social Science and Medicine* 214 (October 2018), https://doi.org/10.1016/j.socscimed.2018.07.014.

17 Roosbelinda Cárdenas et al., '"It's Something That Marks You": Abortion Stigma after Decriminalization in Uruguay', *Reproductive Health* 15, no. 150 (2018), https://doi.org/10.1186/s12978-018-0597-1; Amanda Gelman et al., 'Abortion Stigma Among Low-Income Women Obtaining Abortions in Western Pennsylvania: A Qualitative Assessment', *Perspectives on Sexual and Reproductive Health* 49, no. 1 (2017), https://doi.org/10.1363/psrh.12014; Franz Hanschmidt et al., 'Abortion Stigma: A Systematic Review', *Perspectives on Sexual and Reproductive Health* 48, no. 4 (2016), https://doi.org/10.1363/48e8516; Erick Kiprotich Yegon et al., 'Understanding Abortion-Related Stigma and Incidence of Unsafe Abortion: Experiences from Community Members in Machakos and Trans Nzoia Counties Kenya', *Pan African Medical Journal* 24 (July 2016), https://doi.org/10.11604/pamj.2016.24.258.7567.

18 Ipas, 'Abortion Stigma Ends Here: A Toolkit for Understanding and Action', 2018, https://www.ipas.org/wp-content/uploads/2021/09/Abortion-stigma-ends-here-ABSTTKE18.pdf (accessed 17 July 2022); Sea Change Program, 'Abortion Stigma', 2020, http://www.seachangeprogram.org/ (accessed 8 September 2023).

19 Ipas, 'Abortion Stigma Ends Here'.

20 Fiona K. Bloomer, Kellie O'Dowd and Catriona Ida Macleod, 'Breaking the Silence on Abortion: The Role of Adult Community Abortion Education in Fostering Resistance to Norms', *Culture, Health and Sexuality* 19, no. 7 (2017), https://doi.org/10.1080/13691058.2016.1257740.

21 Wasim Ahmed, 'Public Health Implications of #ShoutYourAbortion', *Public Health* 163 (October 2018), https://doi.org/10.1016/j.puhe.2018.06.010.

22 Patrick W. Corrigan et al., 'Challenging the Public Stigma of Mental Illness: A Meta-Analysis of Outcome Studies', *Psychiatric Services* 63, no. 10 (2012),

https://doi.org/10.1176/appi.ps.201100529; Kathleen M. Griffiths et al., 'Effectiveness of Programs for Reducing the Stigma Associated with Mental Disorders: A Meta-Analysis of Randomized Controlled Trials', *World Psychiatry* 13, no. 2 (2014), https://doi.org/10.1002/wps.20129.

23   Margit Endler et al., 'Telemedicine for Medical Abortion: A Systematic Review', *British Journal of Obstetrics and Gynaecology* 126, no. 9 (2019): 1094, https://doi.org./10.1111/1471-0528.15684.

24   Laura Silver et al., 'Mobile Divides in Emerging Economies', Pew Research Centre, 20 November 2019, https://www.pewresearch.org/internet/2019/11/20/mobile-divides-in-emerging-economies/ (accessed 21 September 2022).

25   Tinus Kruger and Karina Landman, 'Crime and Public Transport: Designing a Safer Journey', Council for Scientific and Industrial Research, Pretoria, 2007, https://researchspace.csir.co.za/dspace/bitstream/handle/10204/1028/Kruger_2007.pdf?sequence=1&isAllowed=y (accessed 27 September 2022).

26   Chiweshe, Mavuso and Macleod, 'Reproductive Justice in Context'.

27   Macleod, Matebese and Tsetse, '"I Drank"'; Matebese, Macleod and Tsetse, 'Shame of Drinking'.

28   Katrina Kimport, Alissa Perrucci and Tracy A. Weitz, 'Addressing the Silence in the Noise: How Abortion Support Talklines Meet Some Women's Needs for Non-Political Discussion of Their Experiences', *Women & Health* 52, no. 1 (2012), https://doi.org/10.1080/03630242.2011.643348.

29   Kate Cockrill and Antonia Biggs, 'Can Stories Reduce Abortion Stigma? Findings from a Longitudinal Cohort Study', *Culture, Health and Sexuality* 20, no. 3 (2018), https://doi.org/10.1080/13691058.2017.1346202; Lisa L. Littman, Christina Zarcadoolas and Adam R. Jacobs, 'Introducing Abortion Patients to a Culture of Support: A Pilot Study', *Archives of Women's Mental Health* 12, no. 6 (2009), https://doi.org/10.1007/s00737-009-0095-0.

30   Madeleine Belfrage, Olivia Ortíz Ramírez and Annik Sorhaindo, 'Story Circles and Abortion Stigma in Mexico: A Mixed-Methods Evaluation of a New Intervention for Reducing Individual Level Abortion Stigma', *Culture, Health and Sexuality* 22, no. 1 (2020), https://doi.org/10.1080/13691058.2019.1577493.

31   For example, Hodes, 'Culture of Illegal Abortion'; Jewkes et al., 'Why Are Women Still Aborting?'.

32   Suzanne Penfold et al., 'A Qualitative Study of Safe Abortion and Post-Abortion Family Planning Service Experiences of Women Attending Private Facilities in Kenya', *Reproductive Health* 15, no. 1 (2018), https://doi.org/10.1186/s12978-018-0509-4.

33   Christina Sathyamala, 'In the Name of Science: Ethical Violations in the ECHO Randomised Trial', *Global Public Health* 17, no. 2 (2022), https://doi.org/10.1080/17441692.2019.1634118.

BIBLIOGRAPHY

Ahmed, Wasim. 'Public Health Implications of #ShoutYourAbortion'. *Public Health* 163 (October 2018): 35–41. https://doi.org/10.1016/j.puhe.2018.06.010.

Albertyn, Cathi. 'Claiming and Defending Abortion Rights in South Africa'. *Revista Direito GV* 11, no. 2 (2015): 429–454. https://doi.org/10.1590/1808-2432201519.

Althaus, Frances A. 'Work in Progress: The Expansion of Access to Abortion Services in South Africa Following Legalization'. *International Family Planning Perspectives* 26, no. 3 (2000): 84–86. https://doi.org/10.2307/2648272.

Amnesty International. 'Barriers to Safe and Legal Abortion in South Africa', 1 February 2017. https://www.amnesty.org/en/documents/afr53/5423/2017/en (accessed 22 February 2022).

Assis, Mariana Prandini and Sara Larrea. 'Why Self-Managed Abortion Is So Much More than a Provisional Solution for Times of Pandemic'. *Sexual and Reproductive Health Matters* 28, no. 1 (2020): 26–29. https://doi.org/10.1080/26410397.2020.17 79633.

Bateman, Chris. 'Abortion Practices Undermining Reformist Laws – Experts: Izindaba'. *South African Medical Journal* 101, no. 5 (2011): 302–304. https://journals.co.za/content/m_samj/101/5/EJC67589 (accessed 11 July 2022).

Bearak, Jonathan, Anna Popinchalk, Bela Ganatra, Ann Beth Moller, Özge Tunçalp, Cynthia Beavin, Lorraine Kwok and Leontine Alkema. 'Unintended Pregnancy and Abortion by Income, Region, and the Legal Status of Abortion: Estimates from a Comprehensive Model for 1990–2019'. *The Lancet Global Health* 8, no. 9 (2020): e1152–e1161. https://doi.org/10.1016/S2214-109X(20)30315-6.

Belfrage, Madeleine, Olivia Ortíz Ramírez and Annik Sorhaindo. 'Story Circles and Abortion Stigma in Mexico: A Mixed-Methods Evaluation of a New Intervention for Reducing Individual Level Abortion Stigma'. *Culture, Health and Sexuality* 22, no. 1 (2020): 96–111. https://doi.org/10.1080/13691058.2019.1577493.

Bertolè, Greta Alice. 'Abortion in South Africa: The Consequences of Conscientious Objection'. *LSE International Development Review* 1, no. 2 (2021). https://idr.lse.ac.uk/articles/abstract/33/ (accessed 15 March 2022).

Bloomer, Fiona K., Kellie O'Dowd and Catriona Ida Macleod. 'Breaking the Silence on Abortion: The Role of Adult Community Abortion Education in Fostering Resistance to Norms'. *Culture, Health and Sexuality* 19, no. 7 (2017): 709–722. https://doi.org/1 0.1080/13691058.2016.1257740.

Bottoman, Esona. 'Pregnant Women's Construction of Social Support from Their Intimate Partners during Pregnancy'. Master's thesis, Rhodes University, Grahamstown, 2018. http://vital.seals.ac.za:8080/vital/access/manager/Repository/vital:28207 (accessed 26 March 2022).

Bradford, Helen. 'Herbs, Knives and Plastic: 150 Years of Abortion in South Africa'. In *Science, Medicine and Cultural Imperialism*, edited by Teresa A. Meade and Mark Walker. London: Palgrave Macmillan, 1991. https://doi.org/10.1007/978-1-349-12445-9_7.

Bridges, John F.P., A. Brett Hauber, Deborah Marshall, Andrew Lloyd, Lisa A. Prosser, Dean A. Regier, F. Reed Johnson and Josephine Mauskopf. 'Conjoint Analysis Applications in Health – a Checklist: A Report of the ISPOR Good Research Practices for Conjoint Analysis Task Force'. *Value in Health* 14, no. 4 (2011): 403–413. https:// doi.org/10.1016/j.jval.2010.11.013.

Burns, Catherine. 'Controlling Birth: Johannesburg, 1920–1960'. *South African Historical Journal* 50, no. 1 (2004): 170–198. https://doi.org/10.1080/02582470409464801.

Cárdenas, Roosbelinda, Ana Labandera, Sarah E. Baum, Fernanda Chiribao, Ivana Leus, Silvia Avondet and Jennifer Friedman. '"It's Something That Marks You": Abortion Stigma after Decriminalization in Uruguay'. *Reproductive Health* 15, no. 150 (2018): 1–11. https://doi.org/10.1186/s12978-018-0597-1.

Chadwick, Rachelle Joy. 'Obstetric Violence in South Africa'. *South African Medical Journal* 106, no. 5 (2016): 423–424.

Chiweshe, Malvern, Jabulile Mavuso and Catriona Ida Macleod. 'Reproductive Justice in Context: South African and Zimbabwean Women's Narratives of Their Abortion Decision'. *Feminism & Psychology* 27, no. 2 (2017): 203–224. https://doi. org/10.1177/0959353517699234.

Clark, Michael and Nolundi Luwaya. 'Communal Land Tenure 1994–2017: Commissioned Report for High Level Panel on the Assessment of Key Legislation and the Acceleration of Fundamental Change, an Initiative of the Parliament of South Africa'. June 2017. Land and Accountability Research Centre, University of Cape Town.

Cockrill, Kate and Antonia Biggs. 'Can Stories Reduce Abortion Stigma? Findings from a Longitudinal Cohort Study'. *Culture, Health and Sexuality* 20, no. 3 (2018): 335–350. https://doi.org/10.1080/13691058.2017.1346202.

Cockrill, Kate and Adina Nack. '"I'm Not That Type of Person": Managing the Stigma of Having an Abortion'. *Deviant Behavior* 34, no. 12 (2013): 973–990. https://doi.org/1 0.1080/01639625.2013.800423.

Cockrill, Kate, Ushma D. Upadhyay, Janet Turan and Diana Greene Foster. 'The Stigma of Having an Abortion: Development of a Scale and Characteristics of Women Experiencing Abortion Stigma'. *Perspectives on Sexual and Reproductive Health* 45, no. 2 (2013): 79–88. https://doi.org/10.1363/4507913.

Constant, Deborah, Daniel Grossman, Naomi Lince and Jane Harries. 'Self-Induction of Abortion among Women Accessing Second-Trimester Abortion Services in the Public Sector, Western Cape Province, South Africa: An Exploratory Study'. *South African Medical Journal* 104, no. 4 (2014): 302–304. https://doi.org/10.7196/ SAMJ.7408.

Corrigan, Patrick W., Scott B. Morris, Patrick J. Michaels, Jennifer D. Rafacz and Nicolas Rüsch. 'Challenging the Public Stigma of Mental Illness: A Meta-Analysis of Outcome Studies'. *Psychiatric Services* 63, no. 10 (2012): 963–973. https://doi.org/10.1176/appi.ps.201100529.

De Bekker-Grob, Esther W. 'Discrete Choice Experiments in Health Care'. PhD thesis, Erasmus University, Rotterdam, 2009. https://doi.org/10.1136/bmj.328.7436.360.

De Bruyn, Maria. 'Women, Reproductive Rights and HIV/AIDS: Issues on Which Research and Interventions Are Still Needed'. *Journal of Health, Population and Nutrition* 24, no. 4 (2006): 413–425. http://www.ncbi.nlm.nih.gov/pmc/articles/pmc3001145/.

DEDEAT (Department of Economic Development, Environmental Affairs and Tourism). 'The Eastern Cape Socio-Economic Review and Outlook', 2017. https://ecsecc.org/infocentre (accessed 21 September 2022).

De Gruchy, John W. 'Calvin(ism) and Apartheid in South Africa in the Twentieth Century: The Making and Unmaking of a Racial Ideology'. In *Calvin and His Influence, 1509–2009*, edited by Irena Backus and Philip Benedict. Oxford: Oxford University Press, 2011. https://doi.org/10.1093/acprof:oso/9780199751846.003.0016.

Dennis, Amanda, Kelly Blanchard and Tshego Bessenaar. 'Identifying Indicators for Quality Abortion Care: A Systematic Literature Review'. *Journal of Family Planning and Reproductive Health Care* 43, no. 1 (2017): 7–15. https://doi.org/10.1136/jfprhc-2015-101427.

Devereux, George. *A Study of Abortion in Primitive Societies*. New York: International Universities Press, 1976.

DiAngelo, Robin and Özlem Sensoy. *Is Everyone Really Equal? An Introduction to Key Concepts in Social Justice Education*. 2nd ed. New York: Teachers College Press, 2017.

Dickson, Kim Eva, Rachel K. Jewkes, Heather Brown, Jonathan Levin, Helen Rees and Luyanda Mavuya. 'Abortion Service Provision in South Africa Three Years after Liberalization of the Law'. *Studies in Family Planning* 34, no. 4 (2003): 277–284. https://doi.org/10.1111/j.1728-4465.2003.00277.x.

Dickson-Tetteh, Kim and Deborah L. Billings. 'Abortion Care Services Provided by Registered Midwives in South Africa'. *International Family Planning Perspectives* 28, no. 3 (2002): 144–150. https://doi.org/10.2307/3088257.

Dijkstra, Lewis, Ellen Hamilton and Sameh Wahba. 'How Do We Define Cities, Towns, and Rural Areas?' *World Bank Blogs: Sustainable Cities*, 10 March 2020. https://blogs.worldbank.org/sustainablecities/how-do-we-define-cities-towns-and-rural-areas (accessed 14 July 2022).

Drisko, James and Tina Maschi. *Content Analysis*. Oxford: Oxford University Press, 2016.

Ebonwu, Joy, Alexandra Mumbauer, Margot Uys, Milton L. Wainberg and Andrew Medina-Marino. 'Determinants of Late Antenatal Care Presentation in Rural and Peri-Urban Communities in South Africa: A Cross-Sectional Study'. *PLOS ONE* 13, no. 3 (2018): 1–16. https://doi.org/10.1371/journal.pone.0191903.

Endler, Margit, Antonella Lavelanet, Amanda Cleeve, Bela Ganatra, Rebecca Gomperts and Kristina Gemzell-Danielsson. 'Telemedicine for Medical Abortion: A Systematic Review'. *British Journal of Obstetrics and Gynaecology* 126, no. 9 (2019): 1094–1102. https://doi.org/10.1111/1471-0528.15684.

Erdman, Joanna N., Kinga Jelinska and Susan Yanow. 'Understandings of Self-Managed Abortion as Health Inequity, Harm Reduction and Social Change'. *Reproductive Health Matters* 26, no. 54 (2018): 13–19. https://www.jstor.org/stable/26605082 (accessed 24 July 2022).

Espinoza, Cecilia, Ghazaleh Samandari and Kathryn Andersen. 'Abortion Knowledge, Attitudes and Experiences among Adolescent Girls: A Review of the Literature'. *Sexual and Reproductive Health Matters* 28, no. 1 (2020). https://doi.org/10.1080/26 410397.2020.1744225.

Favier, Mary, Jamie M.S. Greenberg and Marion Stevens. 'Safe Abortion in South Africa: "We Have Wonderful Laws but We Don't Have People to Implement Those Laws"'. *International Journal of Gynecology and Obstetrics* 143, suppl. 4 (October 2018): 38–44. https://doi.org/10.1002/ijgo.12676.

Feltham-King, Tracey and Catriona Ida Macleod. 'Gender, Abortion and Substantive Representation in the South African Newsprint Media'. *Women's Studies International Forum* 51 (July–August 2015): 10–18. https://doi.org/10.1016/j.wsif.2015.04.001.

Feltham-King, Tracey and Catriona Ida Macleod. 'Multi-Layered Risk Management in Under-Resourced Antenatal Clinics: A Scientific-Bureaucratic Approach versus Street-Level Bureaucracy'. *Health, Risk & Society* 22, no. 1 (2020): 31–52. https://doi. org/10.1080/13698575.2019.1697432.

Fiala, Christian and Joyce H. Arthur. '"Dishonourable Disobedience": Why Refusal to Treat in Reproductive Healthcare Is Not Conscientious Objection'. *Woman – Psychosomatic Gynaecology and Obstetrics* 1 (December 2014): 12–23. https://doi. org/10.1016/J.WOMAN.2014.03.001.

Fitzgerald, Mary. 'How US Anti-Abortion Groups Are Funding South Africa's "Pregnancy Crisis Centres"'. Bhekisisa Centre for Journalism, 17 February 2020. https:// bhekisisa.org/opinion/2020-02-17-how-us-anti-abortion-groups-are-funding-south-africas-pregnancy-crisis-centres/ (accessed 24 July 2022).

Foster, Diana Greene. *The Turnaway Study: Ten Years, a Thousand Women, and the Consequences of Having – or Being Denied – an Abortion*. New York: Scribner, 2020.

Gelman, Amanda, Elian A. Rosenfeld, Cara Nikolajski, Lori R. Freedman, Julia R. Steinberg and Sonya Borrero. 'Abortion Stigma Among Low-Income Women Obtaining Abortions in Western Pennsylvania: A Qualitative Assessment'. *Perspectives on Sexual and Reproductive Health* 49, no. 1 (2017): 29–36. https://doi.org/10.1363/psrh.12014.

Gerdts, Caitlin, Teresa DePiñeres, Selma Hajri, Jane Harries, Altaf Hossain, Mahesh Puri, Divya Vohra and Diana Greene Foster. 'Denial of Abortion in Legal Settings'. *Journal of Family Planning and Reproductive Health Care* 41, no. 3 (2015): 161–163. https:// doi.org/10.1136/jfprhc-2014-100999.

Gerdts, Caitlin, Sarah Raifman, Kristen Daskilewicz, Mariette Momberg, Sarah Roberts and Jane Harries. 'Women's Experiences Seeking Informal Sector Abortion Services in Cape Town, South Africa: A Descriptive Study'. *BMC Women's Health* 17, no. 95 (2017): 1–10. https://doi.org/10.1186/s12905-017-0443-6.

Goffman, Erving. *Stigma: Notes on the Management of Spoiled Identity*. Englewood Cliffs, N.J.: Prentice-Hall, 1963.

Gold, Rachel Benson and Elizabeth Nash. 'TRAP Laws Gain Political Traction While Abortion Clinics – and the Women They Serve – Pay the Price'. *Guttmacher Policy Review* 16, no. 2 (2013): 7–12. http://www.guttmacher.org/pubs/gpr/16/2/gpr160207. html (accessed 29 July 2022).

Government of Ireland. Health (Regulation of Termination of Pregnancy) Act No. 31 of 2018. https://www.irishstatutebook.ie/eli/2018/act/31 (accessed 15 June 2023).

Greaves, Lorraine, Natalie Hemsing, Nancy Poole and Renee O'Leary. 'From Fetal Health to Women's Health: Expanding the Gaze on Intervening on Smoking during

Pregnancy'. *Critical Public Health* 26, no. 2 (2016): 230–238. https://doi.org/10.1080
/09581596.2014.968527.

Greene, Saara. 'Becoming Responsible: Young Mothers' Decision-Making Regarding
Motherhood and Abortion'. *Journal of Progressive Human Services* 17, no. 1 (2006):
25–43. https://doi.org/10.1300/J059v17n01.

Griffiths, Kathleen M., Bradley Carron-Arthur, Alison Parsons and Russell Reid. 'Effectiveness of Programs for Reducing the Stigma Associated with Mental Disorders: A
Meta-Analysis of Randomized Controlled Trials'. *World Psychiatry* 13, no. 2 (2014):
161–175. https://doi.org/10.1002/wps.20129.

Grossman, Daniel, C. Finley Baba, Shelly Kaller, M. Antonia Biggs, Sarah Raifman, Tanvi
Gurazada, Sally Rafie, Sarah Averbach, Karen R. Meckstroth, Elizabeth A. Micks,
Erin Berry, Tina R. Raine-Bennett and Mitchell D. Creinin. 'Medication Abortion
with Pharmacist Dispensing of Mifepristone'. *Obstetrics and Gynecology* 137, no. 4
(2021): 613–622. https://doi.org/10.1097/AOG.0000000000004312.

Guttmacher, Sally, Farzana Kapadia, Jim Te Water Naude and Helen de Pinho. 'Abortion
Reform in South Africa: A Case Study of the 1996 Choice on Termination of Pregnancy Act'. *International Perspectives on Sexual and Reproductive Health* 24, no. 4
(1998): 191–194. https://doi.org/10.2307/2991980.

Guttmacher Institute. 'Abortion in Africa: Fact Sheet', March 2018. https://www.guttmacher.
org/sites/default/files/factsheet/ib_aww-africa.pdf (accessed 15 July 2022).

Hanschmidt, Franz, Katja Linde, Anja Hilbert, Steffi G. Riedel-Heller and Anette Kersting.
'Abortion Stigma: A Systematic Review'. *Perspectives on Sexual and Reproductive
Health* 48, no. 4 (2016): 169–177. https://doi.org/10.1363/48e8516.

Harries, Jane and Deborah Constant. 'Providing Safe Abortion Services: Experiences
and Perspectives of Providers in South Africa'. *Best Practice and Research: Clinical
Obstetrics and Gynaecology* 62 (January 2020): 79–89. https://doi.org/10.1016/j.
bpobgyn.2019.05.005.

Harries, Jane, Diane Cooper, Anna Strebel and Christopher J. Colvin. 'Conscientious
Objection and Its Impact on Abortion Service Provision in South Africa: A Qualitative Study'. *Reproductive Health* 11, no. 1 (2014): 11–16. https://doi.org/10.1186/1742-
4755-11-16.

Harries, Jane, Caitlin Gerdts, Mariette Momberg and Diana Greene Foster. 'An Exploratory Study of What Happens to Women Who Are Denied Abortions in Cape Town,
South Africa'. *Reproductive Health* 12, no. 1 (2015): 1–6. https://doi.org/10.1186/
s12978-015-0014-y.

Harries, Jane, Phyllis Orner, Mosotho Gabriel and Ellen Mitchell. 'Delays in Seeking an
Abortion until the Second Trimester: A Qualitative Study in South Africa'. *Reproductive Health* 4, no. 7 (2007). https://doi.org/10.1186/1742-4755-4-7.

Harries, Jane, Kathryn Stinson and Phyllis Orner. 'Health Care Providers' Attitudes
towards Termination of Pregnancy: A Qualitative Study in South Africa'. *BMC Public
Health* 9, no. 1 (January 2009): 296–306. https://doi.org/10.1186/1471-2458-9-296.

Harris, Laura Florence, Jodi Halpern, Ndala Prata, Wendy Chavkin and Caitlin Gerdts.
'Conscientious Objection to Abortion Provision: Why Context Matters'. *Global Public
Health* 13, no. 5 (2018): 556–566. https://doi.org/10.1080/17441692.2016.1229353.

Harrison, Abigail, Elizabeth T. Montgomery, Mark Lurie and David Wilkinson. 'Barriers
to Implementing South Africa's Termination of Pregnancy Act in Rural KwaZulu/
Natal'. *Health Policy and Planning* 15, no. 4 (2000): 424–431.

Hodes, Rebecca. 'The Culture of Illegal Abortion in South Africa'. *Journal of Southern African Studies* 42, no. 1 (2016): 79–93. https://doi.org/10.1080/03057070.2016.1133086.

Hodes, Rebecca. 'The Medical History of Abortion in South Africa, c. 1970–2000'. *Journal of Southern African Studies* 39, no. 3 (2013): 527–542. https://doi.org/10.1080/03057070.2013.824770.

Holland, Jennifer L. 'Abolishing Abortion: The History of the Pro-Life Movement in America'. *American Historian*, November 2016. https://www.oah.org/tah/issues/2016/november/abolishing-abortion-the-history-of-the-pro-life-movement-in-america/ (accessed 17 July 2022).

Ipas. 'Abortion Stigma Ends Here: A Toolkit for Understanding and Action', 2018. https://www.ipas.org/wp-content/uploads/2021/09/Abortion-stigma-ends-here-ABSTTKE18.pdf (accessed 17 July 2022).

Izugbaraa, Chimaraoke O., Rhoune Ochako and Chibuogwu Izugbara. 'Gender Scripts and Unwanted Pregnancy among Urban Kenyan Women'. *Culture, Health and Sexuality* 13, no. 9 (2011): 1031–1045. https://doi.org/10.1080/13691058.2011.598947.

Jeranji, Tiyese. 'Navigating Abortion Barriers in Rural Areas'. *Spotlight*, 12 February 2021. https://www.spotlightnsp.co.za/2021/02/12/navigating-abortion-barriers-in-rural-areas/ (accessed 4 July 2022).

Jewkes, Rachel K., Heather Brown, Kim Dickson-Tetteh, Jonathan Levin and Helen Rees. 'Prevalence of Morbidity Associated with Abortion before and after Legalisation in South Africa'. *British Medical Journal* 324, no. 7348 (2002): 1252–1253. https://doi.org/10.1136/bmj.324.7348.1252.

Jewkes, Rachel K., Tebogo Gumede, Margaret S. Westaway, Kim Dickson, Heather Brown and Helen Rees. 'Why Are Women Still Aborting Outside Designated Facilities in Metropolitan South Africa?' *BJOG: An International Journal of Obstetrics & Gynaecology* 112, no. 9 (2005): 1236–1242. https://doi.org/10.1111/j.1471-0528.2005.00697.x.

Jewkes, Rachel K. and Helen Rees. 'Dramatic Decline in Abortion Mortality Due to the Choice on Termination of Pregnancy Act'. *South African Medical Journal* 95, no. 4 (2005): 250.

Joffe, Carole. *Dispatches from the Abortion Wars: The Costs of Fanaticism to Doctors, Patients, and the Rest of Us.* Boston: Beacon Press, 2010.

Joffe, Carole. *Doctors of Conscience: The Struggle to Provide Abortion before and after Roe v. Wade.* Boston: Beacon Press, 1995.

Jones, Rachel K., Lori F. Frohwirth and Ann M. Moore. '"I Would Want to Give My Child, like, Everything in the World": How Issues of Motherhood Influence Women Who Have Abortions'. *Journal of Family Issues* 29, no. 1 (2007): 79–99. https://doi.org/10.1177/0192513X07305753.

Kaswa, Ramprakash, George F.D. Rupesinghe and Benjamin Longo-Mbenza. 'Exploring the Pregnant Women's Perspective of Late Booking of Antenatal Care Services at Mbekweni Health Centre in Eastern Cape, South Africa'. *African Journal of Primary Health Care & Family Medicine* 10, no. 1 (2018): 1–9. https://doi.org/10.4102/phcfm.v10i1.1300.

Kimport, Katrina, Alissa Perrucci and Tracy A. Weitz. 'Addressing the Silence in the Noise: How Abortion Support Talklines Meet Some Women's Needs for Non-Political Discussion of Their Experiences'. *Women & Health* 52, no. 1 (2012): 88–100. https://doi.org/10.1080/03630242.2011.643348.

Klausen, Susanne M. *Abortion under Apartheid: Nationalism, Sexuality, and Women's Reproductive Rights in South Africa*. Oxford: Oxford University Press, 2015. https://doi.org/10.1017/CBO9781107415324.004.

Klausen, Susanne M. *Race, Maternity, and the Politics of Birth Control in South Africa 1910–39*. Houndmills: Palgrave Macmillan, 2004.

Klausen, Susanne M. "'The Trial the World Is Watching": The 1972 Prosecution of Derk Crichton and James Watts, Abortion, and the Regulation of the Medical Profession in Apartheid South Africa'. *Medical History* 58, no. 2 (2014): 210–229. https://doi.org/10.1017/mdh.2014.6.

Krüger, Frans. 'SA's Rich Bag of Big, Small and Eclectic Community Radio Stations'. *University of the Witwatersrand News*, 16 February 2020. https://www.wits.ac.za/news/latest-news/opinion/2020/2020-02/sas-rich-bag-of-big-small-and-eclectic-community-radio-stations.html (accessed 28 September 2022).

Kruger, Tinus and Karina Landman. 'Crime and Public Transport: Designing a Safer Journey'. Council for Scientific and Industrial Research, Pretoria, 2007. https://researchspace.csir.co.za/dspace/bitstream/handle/10204/1028/Kruger_2007.pdf?sequence=1&isAllowed=y (accessed 27 September 2022).

Kumar, Anuradha. 'Disgust, Stigma, and the Politics of Abortion'. *Feminism and Psychology* 28, no. 4 (2018): 530–538. https://doi.org/10.1177/0959353518765572.

Kumar, Anuradha, Leila Hessini and Ellen M.H. Mitchell. 'Conceptualising Abortion Stigma'. *Culture, Health & Sexuality* 11, no. 6 (2009): 625–639. https://doi.org/10.1080/13691050902842741.

Laldaparsad, Sharthi. 'Urban and Rural Trends in South Africa'. In *Proceedings of the 59th World Statistics Congress of the International Statistical Institute*, 4317–4321. The Hague: ISI, 2013.

Lie, Mabel L.S., Stephen C. Robson and Carl R. May. 'Experiences of Abortion: A Narrative Review of Qualitative Studies'. *BMC Health Services Research* 8, no. 150 (2008). https://doi.org/10.1186/1472-6963-8-150.

Lince-Deroche, Naomi, Tamara Fetters, Edina Sinanovic and Kelly Blanchard. 'Accessing Medical and Surgical First-Trimester Abortion Services: Women's Experiences and Costs from an Operations Research Study in KwaZulu-Natal Province, South Africa'. *Contraception* 96, no. 2 (2017): 72–80. https://doi.org/10.1016/j.contraception.2017.03.013.

Link, Bruce G. and Jo C. Phelan. 'Conceptualizing Stigma'. *Annual Review of Sociology* 27, no. 1 (2001): 363–385. https://doi.org/10.1146/annurev.soc.27.1.363.

Littman, Lisa L., Christina Zarcadoolas and Adam R. Jacobs. 'Introducing Abortion Patients to a Culture of Support: A Pilot Study'. *Archives of Women's Mental Health* 12, no. 6 (2009): 419–431. https://doi.org/10.1007/s00737-009-0095-0.

Luker, Kristin. *Abortion and the Politics of Motherhood*. Berkeley: University of California Press, 1984.

Mackay, Kara Grace. 'Who Sits at the Table? A Female Farm Activist's Experience during the De Doorns Farm Workers Strike, South Africa'. *Revista Brasileira de Educação Do Campo* 3, no. 3 (2018): 937–948. https://doi.org/10.20873/uft.2525-4863.2018v3n3p937.

Macleod, Catriona Ida. *'Adolescence', Pregnancy and Abortion: Constructing a Threat of Degeneration*. London: Routledge, 2011.

Macleod, Catriona Ida, Siân Beynon-Jones and Merran Toerien. 'Articulating Reproductive Justice through Reparative Justice: Case Studies of Abortion in Great Britain and South Africa'. *Culture, Health & Sexuality* 19, no. 5 (2017): 601–615. https://doi. org/10.1080/13691058.2016.1257738.

Macleod, Catriona Ida, Malvern Chiweshe and Jabulile Mavuso. 'A Critical Review of Sanctioned Knowledge Production Concerning Abortion in Africa: Implications for Feminist Health Psychology'. *Journal of Health Psychology* 23, no. 8 (2018): 1096–1109. https://doi.org/10.1177/1359105316644294.

Macleod, Catriona Ida and Tracey Feltham-King. '"Adolescent Pregnancy": Social Problem, Public Health Concern, or Neither?' In *Routledge International Handbook of Women's Sexual and Reproductive Health*, edited by Jane Ussher, Joan Chrisler and Janette Perz, 253–265. Abingdon: Routledge, 2019. https://doi.org/10.4324/97813510 35620-17.

Macleod, Catriona Ida and Tracey Feltham-King. 'Young Pregnant Women and Public Health: Introducing a Critical Reparative Justice/Care Approach Using South African Case Studies'. *Critical Public Health* 30, no. 3 (2020): 319–329. https://doi. org/10.1080/09581596.2019.1573313.

Macleod, Catriona Ida and Jateen Hansjee. 'Men and Talk about Legal Abortion in South Africa: Equality, Support and Rights Discourses Undermining Reproductive "Choice"'. *Culture, Health & Sexuality* 15, no. 8 (2013): 997–1010. https://doi.org/10. 1080/13691058.2013.802815.

Macleod, Catriona Ida, Sibongile Matebese and Nontozamo Tsetse. '"I Drank Because I Wanted to Deal with the Frustration": Explaining Alcohol Consumption during Pregnancy in a Low-Resource Setting – Women's, Partners' and Family Members' Narratives'. *Social Work* 56, no. 1 (2020): 88–96. https://doi.org/10.15270/52-2-792.

Macleod, Catriona Ida and John Hunter Reynolds. 'Reproductive Health Systems Ana-lyses and the Reparative Reproductive Justice Approach: A Case Study of Unsafe Abortion in Lesotho'. *Global Public Health* 17, no. 6 (2021): 801–814. https://doi.org /10.1080/17441692.2021.1887317.

Macleod, Catriona Ida, Lebogang Seutlwadi and Gary Steele. 'Cracks in Reproductive Health Rights: Buffalo City Learners' Knowledge of Abortion Legislation'. *Health SA Gesondheid* 19, no. 1 (2014): 1–10. https://doi.org/10.4102/hsag.v19i1.743.

Macleod, Catriona Ida and Tiffany Tracey. 'A Decade Later: Follow-up Review of South African Research on the Consequences of and Contributory Factors in Teen-aged Pregnancy'. *South African Journal of Psychology* 40, no. 1 (2010): 18–31. https://doi. org/10.1177/008124631004000103.

Macleod, Catriona Ida and Tiffany Tracey. 'Pregnancy among Young Women in South Africa'. In *International Handbook of Adolescent Pregnancy: Medical, Psychosocial, and Public Health Responses*, edited by Andrew Cherry and Mary Dillon, 545–561. Boston: Springer, 2014. https://doi.org/10.1007/978-1-4899-8026-7_30.

Matebese, Sibongile, Catriona Ida Macleod and Nontozamo Tsetse. 'The Shame of Drinking Alcohol While Pregnant: The Production of Avoidance and Ill Health'. *Journal of Women and Social Work* 36, no. 4 (2021): 629–646. https://doi. org/10.1177/0886109920985139.

Mavodza, Constancia, Rebecca Goldman and Bergen Cooper. 'The Impacts of the Global Gag Rule on Global Health: A Scoping Review'. *Global Health Research and Policy* 4, no. 26 (2019). https://doi.org/10.1186/s41256-019-0113-3.

Mavuso, Jabulile Mary-Jane Jace, Ryan du Toit, Catriona Ida Macleod and Marion Stevens. 'Abortion Counselling in South Africa: A Step-by-Step Guide for Providers'. Critical

Studies in Sexualities and Reproduction Research Unit, Rhodes University, 2018. https://srjc.org.za/wp-content/uploads/2017/06/Abortion_Counselling_Guide_ Version_1-1.pdf (accessed 24 June 2023).

Mavuso, Jabulile Mary-Jane Jace and Catriona Ida Macleod. '"Bad Choices": Unintended Pregnancy and Abortion in Nurses and Counsellors' Accounts of Providing Pre-Abortion Counselling'. *Health* 25, no. 5 (2021): 555–573. https://doi.org/10.1177/1363459320988873.

Mavuso, Jabulile Mary-Jane Jace and Catriona Ida Macleod. 'Contradictions in Womxn's Experiences of Pre-Abortion Counselling in South Africa: Implications for Client-Centred Practice'. *Nursing Inquiry* 27, no. 2 (2020): 1–9. https://doi.org/10.1111/nin.12330.

Mitchell, Ellen M.H., Karen Trueman, Mosotho Gabriel and Lindsey B. Bickers Bock. 'Building Alliances from Ambivalence: Evaluation of Abortion Values Clarification Workshops with Stakeholders in South Africa'. *African Journal of Reproductive Health* 9, no. 3 (2005): 89–99. https://doi.org/10.2307/3583415.

Mohamed, Deeqa, Nadia Diamond-Smith and Jesse Njunguru. 'Stigma and Agency: Exploring Young Kenyan Women's Experiences with Abortion Stigma and Individual Agency'. *Reproductive Health Matters* 26, no. 52 (2018): 128–137. https://doi.org/10.1080/09688080.2018.1492285.

Moodley, Jennifer and Victor Shola Akinsooto. 'Unsafe Abortions in a Developing Country: Has Liberalisation of Laws on Abortions Made a Difference?' *African Journal of Reproductive Health* 7, no. 2 (2003): 34–38. https://doi.org/10.2307/3583211.

Morison, Tracy. 'Heterosexual Men and Parenthood Decision Making in South Africa: Attending to the Invisible Norm'. *Qualitative Research* 34, no. 8 (2013): 1125–1144. https://doi.org/10.1177/0192513X13484271.

Morison, Tracy. 'Reproductive Justice: A Radical Framework for Researching Sexual and Reproductive Issues in Psychology'. *Social and Personality Psychology Compass* 15, no. 6 (2021): 1–10. https://doi.org/10.1111/spc3.12605.

Morison, Tracy and Jabulile Mary-Jane Jace Mavuso, eds. *Reproductive Justice: From the Margins to the Centre.* Lanham: Lexington Press, 2022.

Morrell, Robert, Deevia Bhana and Tamara Shefer, eds. *Books and Babies: Pregnancy and Young Parents in Schools.* Cape Town: HSRC Press, 2012.

Morroni, Chelsea, Landon Myer and Kemilembe Tibazarwa. 'Knowledge of the Abortion Legislation among South African Women: A Cross-Sectional Study'. *Reproductive Health* 3, no. 1 (2006): 1–5. https://doi.org/10.1186/1742-4755-3-7.

Mwaba, Kelvin and Pamela Naidoo. 'Knowledge, Beliefs and Attitudes Regarding Abortion in South Africa among a Sample of University Students'. *Journal of Psychology in Africa* 16, no. 1 (2006): 53–58. https://doi.org/10.1080/14330237.2006.10820104.

Nakajubi, Gloria. 'Beware the Charlatan Sangomas'. *Mail & Guardian*, 5 November 2015.

Nelson, Katherine S., Tuan D. Nguyen, Nathan A. Brownstein, Devon Garcia, Hayden C. Walker, Jordan T. Watson and Aote Xin. 'Definitions, Measures, and Uses of Rurality: A Systematic Review of the Empirical and Quantitative Literature'. *Journal of Rural Studies* 82 (February 2021): 351–365. https://doi.org/10.1016/j.jrurstud.2021.01.035.

Ngabaza, Sisa. 'Positively Pregnant: Teenage Women's Experiences of Negotiating Pregnancy with Their Families'. *Agenda: Empowering Women for Gender Equity* 25, no. 3 (2011): 42–51. https://doi.org/10.1080/10130950.2011.610985.

Ngwena, Charles. 'Conscientious Objection and Legal Abortion in South Africa: Delineating the Parameters'. *Journal for Juridical Science* 28, no. 1 (2003): 1–18. https://doi.org/10.4314/jjs.v28i1.27128.

Norris, Alison, Danielle Bessett, Julia R. Steinberg, Megan L. Kavanaugh, Silvia De Zordo and Davida Becker. 'Abortion Stigma: A Reconceptualisation of Constituents, Causes, and Consequences'. *Women's Health Issues* 21, suppl. 3 (2011): S49–S54. https://doi.org/10.1016/j.whi.2011.02.010.

Orner, Phyllis, Maria de Bruyn and Diane Cooper. '"It Hurts, but I Don't Have a Choice, I'm Not Working and I'm Sick": Decisions and Experiences Regarding Abortion of Women Living with HIV in Cape Town, South Africa'. *Culture, Health and Sexuality* 13, no. 7 (2011): 781–795. https://doi.org/10.1080/13691058.2011.577907.

Orner, Phyllis, Maria de Bruyn and Diane Cooper. 'A Qualitative Exploration of HIV-Positive Pregnant Women's Decision-Making Regarding Abortion in Cape Town, South Africa'. *Methods* 7, no. 2 (2010): 44–51.

Patel, Cynthia J. and Trisha Kooverjee. 'Abortion and Contraception: Attitudes of South African University Students'. *Health Care for Women International* 30, no. 6 (2009): 550–568. https://doi.org/10.1080/07399330902886105.

Penfold, Suzanne, Susy Wendot, Inviolata Nafula and Katharine Footman. 'A Qualitative Study of Safe Abortion and Post-Abortion Family Planning Service Experiences of Women Attending Private Facilities in Kenya'. *Reproductive Health* 15, no. 1 (2018): 1–8. https://doi.org/10.1186/s12978-018-0509-4.

Potgieter, Cheryl and Gail Andrews. 'South African Nurses' Accounts for Choosing to Be Termination of Pregnancy Providers'. *Health SA Gesondheid* 9, no. 2 (2004): 20–30. https://doi.org/10.4102/hsag.v9i2.161.

Price, Elizabeth, Leah S. Sharman, Heather A. Douglas, Nicola Sheeran and Genevieve A. Dingle. 'Experiences of Reproductive Coercion in Queensland Women'. *Journal of Interpersonal Violence* 37, no. 5–6 (2022): NP2823–NP2843. https://doi.org/10.1177/0886260519846851.

Pryor, John B., Glenn D. Reeder and Andrew E. Monroe. 'The Infection of Bad Company: Stigma by Association'. *Journal of Personality and Social Psychology* 102, no. 2 (2012): 224–241. https://doi.org/10.1037/a0026270.

Ralph, Lauren, Heather Gould, Anne Baker and Diana Greene Foster. 'The Role of Parents and Partners in Minors' Decisions to Have an Abortion and Anticipated Coping after Abortion'. *Journal of Adolescent Health* 54, no. 4 (2014): 428–434. https://doi.org/10.1016/j.jadohealth.2013.09.021.

Ramiyad, Devashnee and Cynthia J. Patel. 'Exploring South African Adolescents' Knowledge of Abortion Legislation and Attitudes to Abortion: Sexual Status and Gender Differences'. *South African Journal of Child Health* 10, no. 2 (2016): 105–106. https://doi.org/10.7196/sajch.2016.v10i2.1137.

Rees, Helen. 'The Abortion Debate in South Africa'. *Newsletter: Women's Global Network on Reproductive Rights* no. 36 (July–September 1991): 32–35.

Republic of South Africa. Abortion and Sterilization Act No. 2 (1975). https://www.lexisnexis.co.za/__data/assets/pdf_file/0020/820325/Abortion-and-Sterilization-Act-No.-2-of-1975.pdf (accessed 15 June 2023).

Republic of South Africa. Choice on Termination of Pregnancy Act No. 92 (1996). https://www.parliament.gov.za/storage/app/media/ProjectsAndEvents/womens_month_2015/docs/Act92of1996.pdf (accessed 15 June 2023).

Republic of South Africa. Choice on Termination of Pregnancy Amendment Act No. 1 (2008). https://www.gov.za/sites/default/files/gcis_document/201409/a1-08.pdf (accessed 13 June 2023).

Republic of South Africa. Immorality Amendment Act No. 21 (1950). https://en.wikisource. org/wiki/Immorality_Amendment_Act,_1950 (accessed 13 June 2023).

Republic of South Africa. Immorality Amendment Act No. 57 (1969). https://www.gov. za/sites/default/files/gcis_document/201505/act-57-1969.pdf (accessed 13 June 2023).

Republic of South Africa. Population Registration Act No. 30 (1950). https://en.wikisource. org/wiki/Population_Registration_Act,_1950 (accessed 13 June 2023).

Republic of South Africa. Prohibition of Mixed Marriages Act No. 55 (1949). https:// en.wikisource.org/wiki/Prohibition_of_Mixed_Marriages_Act,_1949 (accessed 13 June 2023).

Ross, Loretta J. and Rickie Solinger. *Reproductive Justice*. Berkeley: University of California Press, 2017.

Rowlands, Sam. 'Misinformation on Abortion'. *European Journal of Contraception & Reproductive Health Care* 16, no. 4 (2011): 233–240. https://doi.org/10.3109/1362 5187.2011.570883.

Ruiters, Greg, ed. *The Fate of the Eastern Cape: History, Politics and Social Policy*. Pietermartizburg: University of KwaZulu-Natal Press, 2011.

Russo, Jennefer A., Kristin L. Schumacher and Mitchell D. Creinin. 'Antiabortion Violence in the United States'. *Contraception* 86, no. 5 (2012): 562–566. https://doi. org/10.1016/j.contraception.2012.02.011.

Sathyamala, Christina. 'In the Name of Science: Ethical Violations in the ECHO Randomised Trial'. *Global Public Health* 17, no. 12 (2022): 4014–4029. https://doi. org/10.1080/17441692.2019.1634118.

Sea Change Program. 'Abortion Stigma', 2020. http://www.seachangeprogram.org/ (accessed 8 September 2023).

Selebalo-Bereng, Lebohang and Cynthia Joan Patel. 'Reasons for Abortion: Religion, Religiosity/Spirituality and Attitudes of Male Secondary School Youth in South Africa'. *Journal of Religion and Health* 58, no. 6 (2019): 2298–2312. https://doi. org/10.1007/s10943-017-0547-1.

Shefer, Tamara, Deevia Bhana and Robert Morrell. 'Teenage Pregnancy and Parenting at School in Contemporary South African Contexts: Deconstructing School Narratives and Understanding Policy Implementation'. *Perspectives in Education* 31, no. 1 (2013): 1–10.

Shellenberg, Kristen M., Ann M. Moore, Akinrinola Bankole, Fatima Juarez, Adekunbi Kehinde Omideyi, Nancy Palomino, Zeba Sathar, Susheela Singh and Amy O. Tsui. 'Social Stigma and Disclosure about Induced Abortion: Results from an Exploratory Study'. *Global Public Health* 6, suppl. 1 (2011): S111–S125. https://doi.org/10.1080/ 17441692.2011.594072.

Shellenberg, Kristen M. and Amy O. Tsui. 'Correlates of Perceived and Internalized Stigma among Abortion Patients in the USA: An Exploration by Race and Hispanic Ethnicity'. *International Journal of Gynecology and Obstetrics* 118, suppl. 2 (2012): S152–S159. https://doi.org/10.1016/S0020-7292(12)60015-0.

Sills, Sophie, Chelsea Pickens, Karishma Beach, Lloyd Jones, Octavia Calder-Dawe, Paulette Benton-Greig and Nicola Gavey. 'Rape Culture and Social Media: Young

Critics and a Feminist Counterpublic'. *Feminist Media Studies* 16, no. 6 (2016): 935–951. https://doi.org/10.1080/14680777.2015.1137962.

Silver, Laura, Mara Vogels, Emily A. Mordecai, Jeremiah Cha, Raea Rasmussen and Lee Rainie. 'Mobile Divides in Emerging Economies'. Pew Research Centre, 20 November 2019. https://www.pewresearch.org/internet/2019/11/20/mobile-divides-in-emerging-economies/ (accessed 21 September 2022).

Smith, Benjamin Elliot Yelnosky, Deborah Bartz, Alisa B. Goldberg and Elizabeth Janiak. '"Without Any Indication": Stigma and a Hidden Curriculum within Medical Students' Discussion of Elective Abortion'. *Social Science and Medicine* 214 (October 2018): 26–34. https://doi.org/10.1016/j.socscimed.2018.07.014.

Sooryamoorthy, Radhamany and Mzwandile Makhoba. 'The Family in Modern South Africa: Insights from Recent Research'. *Journal of Comparative Family Studies* 47, no. 3 (2016): 309–321.

Statistics South Africa. 'Living Conditions of Households in South Africa: An Analysis of Household Expenditure and Income Data Using the LCS 2014/2015'. Statistical Release P0310, 2017. https://www.statssa.gov.za/publications/P0310/P03102014.pdf (accessed 21 June 2022).

Sullivan, Marie E., Abigail Harrison, Jane Harries, Namhla Sicwebu, Rochelle K. Rosen and Omar Galárraga. 'Women's Reproductive Decision Making and Abortion Experiences in Cape Town, South Africa: A Qualitative Study'. *Health Care for Women International* 39, no. 11 (2018): 1163–1176. https://doi.org/10.1080/07399332.2017.1400034.

Trueman, Karen A. and Makgoale Magwentshu. 'Abortion in a Progressive Legal Environment: The Need for Vigilance in Protecting and Promoting Access to Safe Abortion Services in South Africa'. *American Journal of Public Health* 103, no. 3 (2013): 397–399. https://ajph.aphapublications.org/doi/full/10.2105/AJPH.2012.301194.

Trumpy, Alexa J. 'Woman vs. Fetus: Frame Transformation and Intramovement Dynamics in the Pro-Life Movement'. *Sociological Spectrum* 34, no. 2 (2014): 163–184. https://doi.org/10.1080/02732173.2014.878624.

Tsheola, Johannes. 'Paradoxes of Gendered Rurality, Women's Non-Economic Constructions, Disempowerment and State Capitalism in South Africa'. *Academic Journal of Interdisciplinary Studies* 3, no. 1 (2014): 315–324. https://doi.org/10.5901/ajis.2014.v3n1p315.

Turner, Katherine L., Alyson G. Hyman and Mosotho C. Gabriel. 'Clarifying Values and Transforming Attitudes to Improve Access to Second Trimester Abortion'. *Reproductive Health Matters* 16, suppl. 31 (2008): 108–116. https://doi.org/10.1016/S0968-8080(08)31389-5.

Van Dyk, Joan. 'Need an Abortion? Find Clinics You Can Trust Here'. *Mail & Guardian*, 24 November 2021. https://mg.co.za/health/2021-11-24-need-an-abortion-find-clinics-you-can-trust-here/ (accessed 18 July 2022).

Verdeja, Ernesto. 'A Critical Theory of Reparative Justice'. *Constellations* 15, no. 2 (2008): 208–222. https://doi.org/10.1111/j.1467-8675.2008.00485.x.

Vetten, Lisa, Rachel K. Jewkes, Romi Sigsworth, Nicola Christofides, Lizle Loots and Olivia Dunseith. 'Tracking Justice: The Attrition of Rape Cases through the Criminal Justice System in Gauteng'. Tshwaranang Legal Advocacy Centre, the South African Medical Research Council and the Centre for the Study of Violence and Reconciliation, 2008. https://www.csvr.org.za/tracking-justice-the-attrition-of-rape-cases-through-the-criminal-justice-system-in-gauteng/ (accessed 1 August 2022).

World Health Organization. 'Abortion'. 25 November 2021. https://www.who.int/news-room/fact-sheets/detail/abortion (accessed 17 July 2022).

Yegon, Erick Kiprotich, Peter Mwaniki Kabanya, Elizabeth Echoka and Joachim Osur. 'Understanding Abortion-Related Stigma and Incidence of Unsafe Abortion: Experiences from Community Members in Machakos and Trans Nzoia Counties Kenya'. *Pan African Medical Journal* 24 (July 2016): 1–9. https://doi.org/10.11604/pamj.2016.24.258.7567.

Zembylas, Michalinos. '"Shame at Being Human" as a Transformative Political Concept and Praxis: Pedagogical Possibilities'. *Feminism and Psychology* 29, no. 2 (2019): 303–321. https://doi.org/10.1177/0959353518754592.

A

abandonment *see* partner abandonment
abortifacients 30–31, 81, 95, 132–133
aborting/terminating a pregnancy
    see pregnancy termination
abortion
    a disputed issue 63–66
    acceptance/acceptability 64, 71, 76,
        135, 141, 144
    access *see* access to abortion
    attitudes towards 73–76
    brief history 5–7
    care attributes 14–16, 115
    coercion 49, 142
    community attitudes 56–77, 135–138
    community support for 67
    consent *see* consent for abortion
    decision-making 18, 38–56, 84, 92, 99,
        110, 133, 138, 141
    economic concerns 51
    illegal 4–7, 23–28, 34–38, 80–81,
        90–91, 95, 98, 109, 131–132, 143
    illegal providers 81, 90–91, 98, 104,
        112, 119, 129, 132, 136
    legal 6, 21–29, 35, 38, 59, 63–64, 109,
        133
    permission 3, 6, 26
        see also consent for abortion
    reasons for 40, 47, 54, 87–88, 104
    reproductive coercion 43, 54
    rights 7

    second trimester 51
    self-managed 34
    stigma *see* stigma
    support for 56
    unsafe *see* unsafe abortions
Abortion and Sterilization Act 6
abortion facilities
    factors in choosing a facility/provider
        115–123
    knowledge of 27–31
    location preferences 121–123
    opening time preferences
        123–125
    stand-alone clinics 121, 127
    type of facility/service preferences
        117–121
abortion information sources 34–38
    preference 126 fig 6.3
    ranking 126 table 6.7
abortion laws/legislation 2, 13
    knowledge of 18, 21–38, 95
    liberalisation 5, 7, 143
abortion procedures 131, 133
    knowledge of 22, 31–34
abortion services
    access *see* access to abortion
    first-trimester 3
    illegal *see* abortion, illegal
    information sources 34–38
    knowledge of 21–38, 112
    legal providers *see* abortion, legal

abortion services (*continued*)
    preferences 114–128, 116–118 fig
      6.1&6.2, 120, 127
    provision 144
    understanding of 13
'Abortion Stigma Ends Here' (Ipas
    manual) 136
access to abortion (services) 1–4, 13, 21,
    27–29, 31, 56, 79, 92, 102, 104–105,
    117, 131–132, 138
    barriers *see* barriers to having an
      abortion
    for rape victims 66
    for women with HIV 36
    impediment 109
    in the Eastern Cape 15
    offence to obstruct legal abortion 25
    right to a safe abortion 19
adoption 21, 71, 105, 108
African National Congress (ANC) 7
Afrikaner nationalist ideologies 5
alcohol use during pregnancy 42
Amathole district municipality
    11–12
Amnesty International 109
ANC *see* African National Congress
antenatal care 18, 51–55, 133, 138
anti-abortion
    activists/advocates/groups 61, 81, 106,
      137
    arguments/rhetoric 57–63, 135
    sentiment(s) 18, 137
    stance 90, 94, 137
anti-abortionists 61, 82
apartheid 5–10
attitudes
    community 18, 56–77, 135–138
    family 40
    healthcare providers/workers 4,
      108–109, 134
    partner 98, 110–112
    towards abortion 76
    towards legal status of abortion 25
    towards pregnancy among teenagers
      73–76
    towards rape victims who abort 66–72
    towards women's autonomy 56

B

Baragwanath Hospital 6
barriers to having an abortion 19, 38,
    97–113, 129
    confidentiality breaches 97
    costs 97, 100–103
    distance 97, 100–103
    fear of abortion or consequences 97,
      105–106
    gestational limits 103–105
    healthcare staff hostility
      106–110
    lack of support 97
    partner attitude 97, 110–111
basic health services 11
    see also health services
Bhekisisa 29
black people/women
    barriers 4
    care after abortion 6
    dying after illegal abortions 7, 129
    knowledge of abortion laws 22
    laws on movement 9
    wealth 37
Bulungula Incubator 12

C

casual sex 40
child-support grant 51, 87
Choice on Termination of Pregnancy Act
    (CTOP Act) 2–4, 7, 21–25, 38–39,
    51, 75, 103–104, 106, 109, 129,
    131–133, 141
Ciskei 9–11
class 84–85, 95, 130
class-based power relations 84–85, 95
Cockrill, Kate 80, 89, 91
collective material dimension 130 fig 7.1,
    131–134
collective symbolic dimension 130 fig 7.1,
    134–138
concealment of abortion/pregnancy
    49–50, 90–95, 112, 136
confidentiality
    agreement 13
    breaches/breaking 93–94, 97–100, 112,
      117, 119, 122

fear of breaches 3–4, 28, 129, 134
health information disclosure 93
imperative/importance of 92, 121,
        123, 134
lack of confidentiality at hospitals 90
maintaining 98–100
oath of 99
versus cost 14, 95–98, 114–128, 134
consent for abortion 6, 139
informed 32, 108
parental 2, 23, 26
spousal 2
contraception 108–109, 120, 133
Covid-19 lockdowns 34
Critical Studies in Sexualities and
        Reproduction 4
CTOP Act see Choice on Termination of
        Pregnancy Act
curettage 7, 31

D
DCE see discrete choice experiment
decision to abort see abortion, decision
        making
denying paternity see paternity denial
Department of Health 4, 51, 133
dilation and curettage 7, 31
disclosure of confidential health
        information 93
discrete choice experiment (DCE) 12,
        14–15, 17 table 0.1, 19, 89, 92,
        114–115, 127, 139, 144
demographics of sample 17 table 0.1
research steps 15 fig 0.2
dynamics (abortion-related)
community dynamics 42
family-related see family-related
        dynamics
gender see gender dynamics
most prominent 41
of class 84
partner-related see partner-related
        dynamics
poverty-related 53
relationship dynamics 47
social see social dynamics
structural see structural dynamics

E
East Cape Agricultural Research Project
        (ECARP) 11
ECARP see East Cape Agricultural
        Research Project
extramarital sex 5

F
family-related dynamics 18, 47–50
disapproval 47–49, 54
physical violence 47
threats 47
violence in the family/home 65
fieldworkers 13, 117, 144
foetal abnormalities 6, 39

G
gender correlation with poverty 9
gender dynamics 43, 142
gendered power relations 38
gestation
age 141
cut-off points/limits 2–3, 22, 25, 27,
        32, 51, 59, 103–105
dating 39, 104, 140
Global Gag Rule 38
Goffman, Erving 79
guardian permission see parental consent
Guttmacher Institute 80

H
Harries, Jane 35, 102, 104, 109
health services 1, 11, 120, 127, 133, 138
hostility 19, 98
HIV 36
as reason for abortion 87–88
care 133
funds 38
stigma 3, 136–137
testing 93
homosexuality 5
hostility towards abortion 19, 98,
        106–109, 112

I
Immorality Amendment Act 5
incest see rape and incest

information channel preferences
125–126
informed consent 32, 108
International Independent Ethics in
Research Committee 13
interpretive content analysis 14
Ipas 108, 136
ISPOR Task Force 14

J
Jezile, Onke 1
Joffe, Carole 81
judgement 86–87, 96, 136, 141
from the community 43, 57, 65, 72, 77,
83, 85–86
judgemental healthcare provider attitudes
109, 134

K
Keiskamma Trust 11–12
Kumar, Anuradha 58–59, 79, 136

L
land tenure 8–10
legislation
abortion *see* abortion laws/legislation
race-based 5
restrictive 34, 66
Lethabo la Azania 1
liberalisation of abortion laws 5, 7, 143
Link, Bruce 80–81, 84

M
Manjezi, Nomthandazo 12
Marie Stopes South Africa (MSSA) 1, 4,
15, 16 fig 0.3, 18, 117
International Independent Ethics in
Research Committee 13
material dimension 130 fig 7.1, 138–141
mifepristone 7, 31
misoprostol 7, 31
mixed-methods approach/research 1, 12
MLR *see* multinomial logistic regression
morbidity and mortality (maternal) 3,
51–52, 106
mortality *see* morbidity and mortality
MSSA *see* Marie Stopes South Africa

multinomial logistic regression (MLR)
coefficients
for facility location 122–123 table 6.3
& 6.4
for opening times 124–125 table 6.5
& 6.6
for services offered 120 table
6.1 & 6.2
multinomial logistic regressions (MLRs)
115
multiple partnerships/relationships 40,
42, 54, 136

N
Nack, Adina 80, 89, 91
non-judgemental healthcare 135, 138
non-judgementalism 76

O
obstetric violence 53, 55, 107
online storytelling 137

P
parental consent 2, 23, 26
partner
abandonment 44–46, 54, 142
attitude 110–112
coercion 46
relationships 54
partner-related dynamics 18–19, 53
partner-related interactions in decision
making 40–47
paternity denial 41–44, 46, 54, 86, 142
perinatal care 51–55
Phelan, Jo 80–81, 84
Population Registration Act 5
post-abortion care/support 130 fig 7.1,
131–133, 142
post-apartheid
commitment to reproductive health
rights 2–3
liberalisation of abortion laws 5, 7
poverty
and gender 9
and lack of antenatal care 18, 54
and the decision to abort 40, 50–51,
53, 138, 141

as reason to terminate a pregnancy
86–88
Eastern Cape 143
-related dynamics 53
pregnancy
abandonment *see* partner
abandonment
accurate detection 104
alcohol use 42
among teenagers 19, 73–77, 136–137
concealing/concealment 49–50, 90–95,
112, 136
decision to abort 3, 21
early detection 39, 139–140
expenses 51
gestation 32
in casual/multiple partnerships 43, 46–47
in school 49
legal termination 22, 39
out of wedlock 58
testing 32, 105, 140
unplanned 41, 44
youthful 48
pregnancy termination
after three months 27
by a minor 23, 26
by a woman 40, 142
by wealthy women 85
cut-off points/limit 59
due to judgement from the
community 43
due to poverty 86–88
due to rape 67–71, 142
economic concerns 51
in first trimester 39
services 29
prenatal care 51–52
pro-choice 58
pro-life 58
production of stigma 80–81
Prohibition of Mixed Marriages Act 5
pronatalist community/culture 62, 71, 141

Q

qualitative research component 12–14, 22
quantitative research component
14–18, 115

R

race 79, 130
race-based legislation 5
rape and incest
abortion acceptance 2, 6, 18–19,
24, 39, 56, 58, 61, 65–70, 76,
135, 142
attitudes towards victims who abort
66–73
community support for abortion
67–68
myths 71–72, 77, 142
trauma 69–71, 76, 142
relationship dynamics 47
religion 56, 79
religious
beliefs/interpretations 57, 80
metaphors 25, 36
qualms 38
reasons for family disapproval 48
sensibilities 49
reparative reproductive justice 129–131
dimensions 130 fig 7.1, 131–143
model 131
reproductive
coercion 43, 54
control 5–7
justice 19, 129–131, 144
services 1, 127, 137–138
research (our) 4, 10–18, 54, 63
components 12
methodology 9
research steps in the DCE 15 fig 0.2
Rhodes University Ethical Standards
Committee 13
rights
abortion 7
knowledge of 111–112
language of 65–66
of people 130, 131
reproductive health 54
to decide outcome of a pregnancy 58
to reproductive healthcare service
2–3
women's 133
Roman-Dutch law 5
rurality 7–10

S

SADHS *see* South African Demographic and Health Survey
sanctity of foetal life 71
Sarah Baartman district municipality 11
self-induction 23, 31, 112
sex
    casual 40
    extramarital 5
    outside of wedlock 136
sex-selective abortion 2
sexual and reproductive control measures 5
sexual and reproductive (health) services 127, 133, 138
sexual violence 141
sexually transmitted infections 133
shame 48–49, 54, 82, 98, 142
Shellenberg, Kristin 82
site sampling 10–12
social dynamics 40, 79, 130 fig 7.1, 141
social parenting 74
Sontuntu, Bongezwa 12
South African Demographic and Health Survey (SADHS) 22
spousal consent 2
stigma 63, 67
    by association 72, 76–77
    community attitudes 135–138
    conceptualising 79–82
    domains 82
    experienced 82–83
    in rural South Africa 78–96
    internalised 89
    major types 79
    management 19, 89–95
    of not having children 62
    perceived 83–88
    production 80–81
    reduction 137
    theories/theory 80
stigmatisation/stigmatising 79, 112
    by partner(s) 84, 112
    by teachers 49
    of women who abort 95
STIs 133

structural dynamics 130 fig 7.1, 141
studies on abortion decision making 44
study (this)
    findings 19, 129, 131
    pilot study 13
    sites 11 fig 0.1
    strengths and limitations 143–144
support talklines 142
symbolic dimension 130 fig 7.1, 141–143

T

talklines 142
teenagers
    attitudes towards pregnancy 73–76
    knowledge of abortion 22
    pregnancies/pregnancy 19, 48, 77, 136
terminating a pregnancy
        see aborting/terminating a pregnancy
traditional healers 112, 117, 119, 132–133
    abortions 3, 29–30, 38
Tranükul P 10, 12
trauma of rape 69–71, 76, 142
Triad Trust 29
Trump, Donald 38
Tsheola, Johannes 9
Tsui, Amy 82
Turnaway Study (USA) 51

U

ukubukuzana 45
ukwaliswa 45
unsafe abortions 119, 131–132
    consequences 106
    deaths 63, 104
    practices/services 143
    risks 34, 96, 132

V

vacuum aspiration 7, 31
value clarification and attitude transformation workshops 108
viability 59